100 Songs
for Eternity

AF191724

MUSIC WAS MY FIRST LOVE,
AND IT WILL BE MY LAST ...

(JOHN MILES - MUSIC)

Ferdinand Köther

100 Songs
for Eternity

An audiobook for reading

Bibliographic information of the German National Library: The German National Library lists this publication in the German National Bibliography; detailed bibliographic data is available online at dnb.dnb.de.

Publisher: BoD · Books on Demand GmbH,
In de Tarpen 42, 22848 Norderstedt, bod@bod.de
Printed by: Libri Plureos GmbH, Friedensallee 273, 22763 Hamburg

ISBN: 978-3-7693-7741-5

The playlist for "100 Songs for Eternity" can be found on Spotify® and Tidal® under its German name "100 Songs für die Ewigkeit", featuring almost all these songs, though in a few cases unfortunately in different versions—or not at all. Different versions also mean, in at least one case, a different artist (on Tidal).

INTRODUCTION

This is an audiobook for reading – ideally, the reader has the song in their archive or can download and listen to it while reading, either before or after.

By "song", incidentally, I always mean this version, even if it is usually, but not always, the first original recording of the composition. But what is a song without interpreters? A piece of paper with notes on it, if at all. A song only breathes life through its interpretation, and so here it is also about the musicians, not least the composers... but last, unfortunately, as this would exceed the scope.

Composers are rarely in the spotlight but can console themselves with the fact that they often can claim the majority of the royalties to their account, rightfully so. Moreover, "song" for me means that it is a piece of music that lingers in the ear due to the melody, sometimes just because of the rhythm and/or the combination of these two elements, and above all the dedication of the artist (by which individuals and groups are meant). "Song" generally means a piece of music with vocals, which applies to the vast majority presented here, and as always, exceptions prove the rule.

The selection and almost everything written here is subjective, but it may also offer the opportunity for some readers/listeners to delve deeper into this or that artist or song, or to remember, back then...

Nevertheless, I have tried to incorporate a certain objectivity regarding the significance of these or at least some pieces of music and also musicians in the history of music. There may and should be shared opinions on this, ultimately (almost) everything is a matter of taste.

That's good, and those who share my taste and perhaps especially those who do not, may discover or rediscover some things here.

And what is my taste? Clearly on the heavy/hard rock side, but also with a great inclination towards melody and emotions, and who says that emotions cannot be heavy? And how so...

100 Songs for Eternity could also be 100 Beatles songs, which I deliberately did not consider. In fact all Beatles songs are an eternal heritage.

The Beatles are the gods of Olympus, upon whom all other music demigods and heroes wanted to ascend and without whom they would not exist, at least not in this form and manner (and the Beatles could not have climbed the summit of Olympus without some preceding music demigods and heroes, at least not in this form and manner).

That's what I claim, and it may sound strange with my heavy preference, but it is so. Period. Different topic. Period. And who says anyway that the Beatles are not heavy, in every respect?

Nevertheless, we will encounter the Beatles here and there, how could the earth be without the sky? My "taste'" largely ends in the 1980s, this as a "warning". So, this selection of songs, including some "standards", predominantly offers a retrospective of the 1960s to 1980s of the last century (and a bit of 21st century), with the 60s being the most innovative decade for ages and unsurpassed since, I claim as a rock grandpa.

I consider the ability to describe songs in words to be limited – the reader/listener may forgive me for some, hopefully not too many, repetitions, but this book should not necessarily be read/listened to in order from A-Z.

Therefore, often little is written about the song itself and I try to awaken interest with references to the artist themselves and also to other songs and artists and background information and other ramblings, to delve deeper into this or that group or artist or song and the history of music in general. Sometimes the enthusiasm may get the better of me, but that's good – music is passion and enthusiasm, and everyone feels it differently.

Some will surely think from time to time "oh, this bloody old stuff again", some especially young readers may have never heard this old stuff before. Doesn't matter, I hope this small selection of songs may inspire some to delve deeper into the wonderful world of music. There are many more (at least) songs for eternity that everyone may discover for themselves. Have fun with it!

But now, put your headphones on (preferably), turn the volume up LOUD, and off you go!

And it is as banal as timeless:

KEEP ON ROCKIN'!

Notes on notation: I first mention the song title, then the performer, and below, the composer(s) in parentheses. The generally common, but not always consistent, notation is music composer/lyric composer. I always separated all names with a comma, often the distinction between music and lyric composer is not clear (in the book text, however, if mentioned, written as x/y, as a comma at this point would impair readability).

The songs are alphabetically ordered by title, according to the index in the appendix with the names of the performers. There is also an index of the performers in alphabetical order (without the song titles and without "The", as indicated for some groups where it seemed appropriate) incorporating the first name for the first letter – contrary to my habit.

In the text, the song title is written in **bold**, as in the heading, other mentioned songs or album titles are written in *italics*. The performer itself and other performers are not highlighted in the text. [A few current additions, made during the proofreading or this post-production in 2023, are placed in square brackets.]

I deliberately did not include years with the title; sometimes in the text, the same goes for references to albums. This book is/was supposed to be an incentive to delve deeper into the subject, I have already said so. Everyone has internet access, everyone can and should use it wisely.

[See the imprint for playlists related to this book.]
Wikipedia is a great source of information, to which I owe some of the information mentioned here and have compiled it because I might have forgotten or didn't know it at all. My sincere thanks to Wikipedia (which everyone should support with a small donation from time to time).

The length of a (my) text, by the way, has nothing to do with the (subjective) quality and appreciation of the song.

Thanks to Chat GPT – faster than me, quite as good, only few alterations were needed.

AEGIAN SEA - APHRODITE'S CHILD

(Vangelis Papathanassiou, Costas Ferris)

Aphrodite's Child, weren't they those Greeks with the cheesy canoodle song *Rain and Tears*? Yes, that's right, they were "those Greeks," especially Demis Roussos with his disarming voice and Vangelis Papathanassiou, who later had a successful solo career as a keyboardist under the simple name "Vangelis," just like his colleague Demis Roussos as a singer and heartthrob for (house)wives – don't get me wrong, I don't want to offend either him or housewives or women in general (on the contrary). And I also liked *Rain and Tears*.

I have to digress here – this song comes from the concept album *666* (double LP from 1971, later 2-CD), which could also be called a rock opera (I hate that term because I hate operas). *666* (The Number of the Beast – the official subtitle is *The Apocalypse of John, 13/18*) is a remarkable, little-known, and sometimes hard-to-digest opus.

Irene Papas' screaming/moaning in ∞ (that's the name of the song) makes Jane Birkin's *Je t'aime* sound like happy baby talk.

Although or perhaps precisely because taken out of context, **Aegian Sea** is an absolutely outstanding piece of music for me. On floating synth sounds, accompanied by a beautiful bass line and choir singing, follows a "drumbeat" (drums) and a cascading downward sequence of notes... repeat the whole thing... and again... if anyone finds this boring, yawning or falling asleep by then, I won't argue with them, but recommend they keep listening (if they haven't already fallen asleep). On the third time, when you're waiting for the drumbeat (if...), a beautiful guitar (I think so, could also be a synth?) with heavenly sound begins and a deep male voice (not Demis Roussos) starts to briefly and succinctly tell the story of the end of the world – not singing! A little later, a wonderfully creaking-sawing synth sound (I'm sure of that) joins in the background, and with this heavenly guitar, everything merges into a wonderfully... heavenly sound, in stark contrast to the spoken text.

Music is often difficult to describe in words, and this is once again particularly true in this case.

A calm and very atmospheric song that you must let work on yourself and that strongly affects the emotions if you are receptive to it. Strangely, a little bit of *Rain and Tears* cheesiness comes through, and I estimate that this is one of my highly personal eternal songs for which "no pig cares".

But pigs are intelligent and capable of learning, especially those who read books...

By the way, in correct English it should be "Aegean Sea"; whether this deviation was intentional or a "typo," I don't know.

Anyway, Demis and Vangelis were much more successful commercially later on. But none of their songs ever touched me as deeply as Aegean

Sea (correctly spelled), and I am delightedly diving into the eternity of the Aegean Sea (despite the un-delightful lyrics)!

AIN'T NO SUNSHINE - MAMA LION
(Bill Withers)

I confess – like many others, my first attention was drawn to Mama Lion's album *Preserve Wildlife* because of the cover. The attractive blonde with a slight silver gaze, looking seductively, was definitely an eye-catcher, especially when you open the grid window of the cover and see her holding a lion cub to her opulent bare chest. You'd want to be wildlife yourself.

With this beautiful fold-out cover, you probably could avoid being "not suitable for youth" and stimulate curiosity. Sex sells... or maybe not, as the album and the Mama Lion project as such didn't achieve great success. Perhaps this display was even counterproductive, as many may have thought, "well, she's pretty, but there's probably not much substance there."

Far from it! There's not just something for your eyes, but also something to blow your ears. Californian rock singer Lynn Carey, who shows off her daring nature behind the cover grid so impressively, and Canadian multi-talented musician Neil Merryweather (who has his own entry in this book) had already collaborated before forming the group Mama Lion. Lynn is occasionally compared to Janis Joplin, but why make comparisons? Both women could be proud to be compared to each other.

Their introduction to the first song on the album, with Neil's bass gently adding in (and later, of course, other instruments), kicks off and doesn't let up – the lioness roars, and Mama Lion turn this wonderful, lightly jazzy song into a strong piece of rock/blues rock that hits hard. This continues throughout this album as well as their second and unfortunately last album.

Ain't No Sunshine is probably one of the most covered songs, and in this case Wikipedia has some big gaps to fill. Often, as mentioned before, it's jazz-influenced, soulful and/or presented in a lounge style, but never as racy as it is here, without losing the character of the song. The late Bill Withers would have probably appreciated this interpretation of his brilliant composition.

And if not – Wildlife is definitely worth preserving, not just when it's presented visually and, above all, acoustically like this by Mama Lion. A lioness for eternity, even if there's probably no sunshine there!

ALL ALONG THE WATCHTOWER - JIMI HENDRIX EXPERIENCE

(Bob Dylan)

Two icons in one fell swoop – Jimi, the guitar master of all classes, trailblazer and innovator with immeasurable influence on generations of musicians, and Bob, actually Robert, a great lyricist and composer, with a similarly great impact and lasting significance, now also a Nobel laureate.

Looking at it the other way around – Jimi has composed some classic songs, while Bob as a musician has also delivered some nice tunes, but otherwise is more of an "afterthought" for me. The Zimmermans (Dylan followers – Robert Allen Zimmerman is his real name) will stone me, but I can handle it, like a rolling stone...

Jimi made every piece of music "his piece of music" with his guitar and unique singing style (or even without singing, like the American national anthem *Star Spangled Banner*), first demonstrated with his first big hit *Hey Joe*, an ancient standard, from then on a "Hendrix song". Jimi didn't just interpret the songs, he completely made them his own and gave them a new, completely different life.

This also applies to this song, many people only know **All Along The Watchtower** as a "Hendrix song", which does great injustice to the brilliant composer.

Two geniuses working together create something new, each contributing their own unique aspect. Like many Dylan songs, this one has been interpreted by many other artists, but never as penetrating, heavy and at the same time floating as by Jimi. The fantasy text is reminiscent of early King Crimson lyrics, or vice versa, **All Along The Watchtower** came earlier.

Writing more about Jimi Hendrix would be more than futile, there are hardly any other artists with more publications, except for the Beatles. And with hardly any other artist's legacy, or none at all, has more mischief been done, that's another story. This doesn't mean that there aren't some gems to be found among his estate.

Always along the wall... no, always along the watchtower, for eternity, into which Jimi entered much too early and which he probably thoroughly dominates with his guitar. Nothing better could happen to it.

ALL THE WAY FROM MEMPHIS - MOTT THE HOOPLE

(Ian Hunter)

Motze... who? Some may ask this question if they are not familiar with the band named after a novel (not by Charles Dickens or J.R.R. Tolkien, but by Willard Manus). Alright, I don't know that novel either (maybe a failure?), but I do know this great band very well, which reached its peak during the glam rock era of the 70s.

Their good debut album with the fantastic Hieronymus Bosch cover and the stunning instrumental version (!) of *You Really Got Me* (see there) attracted attention and created a small fan community, but just like their following, quite remarkable albums, it didn't lead to a breakthrough.

It wasn't until David Bowie composed *All The Young Dudes* for them while they were considering their dissolution out of frustration, that things started to take off. Bowie and Mott The Hoople somehow fit together well, both being stylistically chameleon-like, very changeable and colourful. Bowie himself recorded this song only much later, almost "incidentally", but often performed it live; there is a version with Mott The Hoople and David Bowie performing it together.

Anyway, suddenly Mott The Hoople were "in demand" and produced some great hits, transforming from a long-haired hippie rock band to a still long-haired, stylized glam rock band, led by the always sunglass-wearing, charismatic singer Ian Hunter. Not only he knew how to control his voice, but also the other guys had nothing to hide from anyone.

Their mentioned great hits are all similar in a way, they had found their successful formula, triggered by *All The Young Dudes*. Which one should I choose here... *Honaloochie Boogie*, *The Golden Age Of Rock 'n' Roll* or maybe *Roll Away The Stone*?

No, **All The Way From Memphis** (strangely also called *All the Way To Memphis* sometimes) is the essence of their sound during those successful years: the wonderfully rolling honky-tonk piano intro immediately gets you moving and sets the equally wonderful rolling rhythm. Then Ian Hunter's singing skills come in, a strong guitar in the background, also some saxophone – rock 'n' roll, in short. During the solo, saxophone and guitar alternate, the honky-tonk piano is always audible, just like everything else. That rocks!

The way from Memphis may take a long time, but we have enough time for this wonderful song, until the end of eternity.

A WHITER SHADE OF PALE -
PROCOL HARUM

(Gary Brooker, Keith Reed, Matthew Fisher)

Can you bathe in tones? I certainly can, especially in guitar tones, but organ tones are also well-suited for it, if they have that "bathing sound".

I was never an enthusiastic churchgoer; as a little boy, it was simply something you were "forced" to do without enthusiasm, as an altar boy it wasn't quite as boring, then not at all anymore – but a small glimmer of hope was usually the roaring organ sound, which made the stay a little less boring.

But never did any organ sound more heavenly than in this mega-hit of the year 1967, still one of the ultimate love songs of all time, as more than 10 million singles sold are a clear proof (not many singles have achieved that). Presumably, at least temporarily, many singles also became "twingles" as a result...

Classically influenced, with a slight blues rhythm and Gary Brooker's unmistakable voice, this incomparable melody sneaks into every pore of your skin, hair and heart, and strangely enough fits perfectly into the flower power era, not least because of the nonsensical fantasy lyrics. LSD in musical form, but in this form, it lasts forever.

It would be very unfair to reduce Procol Harum to this song, they have delivered many excellent albums with often very complex songs, often with that certain classical touch and more and more with Robin Trower's unique guitar playing in the foreground – he then embarked on a great solo career. (And is also represented in this book.)

Nevertheless, the name Procol Harum cannot shake off the "blemish" of forever being synonymous with this unmatched soft rock ("fabric softener") giant – a blemish that many others would like to have.

The record for the most misspelled name is also not to be taken away from them (mostly "Procul Harum", or "Procul Harem", etc.).

BAKER STREET - GERRY RAFFERTY

(G. Rafferty)

The "street of bakers" in London is nothing special, pretty long like many streets in London, that's it... almost.

The same goes, incidentally, for *Penny Lane* in Liverpool, which had the honour of being the title of a Beatles song, but that's another story... In song titles, there are some streets, or roads (e.g. to Cairo, Julie Driscoll with Brian Auger & Trinity or to Hell, Chris Rea), but rarely existing ones.

The **Baker Street** became famous thanks to Gerry Rafferty's song, a huge worldwide hit. The Beatles had their Apple Boutique and offices there, Ringo's former apartment is nearby where John and Jimi Hendrix also lived, but those are other stories again.

Nowadays, there is at least a fairly large official Beatles shop there (not in the former boutique location), and if you want to go to Madame Tussaud's, you take the tube to **Baker Street**, which may cause some confusion – the wax figures reside on Marylebone Road. If I'll ever have nothing to do, I'll become a tour guide in London... so never.

Gerry doesn't deal with these facts in his song, rather he was there often at his lawyer's during legal battles with his former band Stealers Wheel (nice, but never really my thing) and also liked to drink too much... too much, which later led to his relatively early death.

The loose and casual song is more about these circumstances (except for death), somewhat hidden and packaged in a grand melody.

The unspectacular but very pleasant voice of the Scot is embedded in a sound package of a spectacular saxophone riff (which sounds almost like a guitar), a fantastic guitar solo and occasional, light background "growling" in the transitions, which I can only assume was somehow generated with keyboards. If you know exactly, you can let me know.

This impressive blend smoothly, and casually, brilliantly paves the auditory canals, and even though **Baker Street** is not the longest street, it leads directly into eternity.

BEDS ARE BURNING - MIDNIGHT OIL
(Rob Hirst, Jim Moginie, Peter Garrett)

The success of this band from Uluruland (Australia) in the 80s somehow passed me by, but fortunately I discovered them later. Their hearty, very special mix of rock, pop, and other styles mostly goes straight to your legs, but should also go into your brain.

The often political and socially critical lyrics are not always easy for non-Aussies to understand, but it's worth reading them. Especially **Beds Are Burning** – it doesn't point fingers, but already showed enormous foresight in 1987. The pumping rhythm and accentuated breaks support the theme perfectly, not least the ticking clock imitating percussion beats.

"How can we sleep while our beds are burning?" "It's time to pay our dues." That is more relevant than ever nowadays and it's amazing that Midnight Oil had already recognized where the journey was going during times of carefree abundance. Due to their political and critical attitude, they weren't exactly a media darling; maybe that's why they slipped through my fingers at the time.

The charismatic singer Peter Garrett later became the Australian environment minister, also took over other departments, and nowadays tours again with Midnight Oil on stages around the world, if I am informed correctly.

The tours are certainly sustainable, and a new album is also announced – this time I won't miss anything. My rare promo CD (with 25 partly rare pieces/versions, a special treasure) from the early 90s bears the imprint "This wrapper is manufactured from 100% recycled paper." No plastic, apart from the CD itself, just paper and cardboard and at the time a still largely unknown hint. A wonderful, 8-minute version of **Beds Are**

Burning is the highlight. The inlay says "this is a fragile ball we are living on and we are destroying it." I'm repeating myself: late 80s, early 90s!

Our ball doesn't last forever, but this song will echo forever, even if no one can hear it anymore. All admonishing words are in vain, and with such a band and such a song, the contemplation can also be a little more binding. Our beds have been burning for a long time, but as long as they are not completely burned down, we can and should enjoy this poignant work despite its depressing message.

BLACK HOLE SUN - SOUNDGARDEN
(Chris Cornell)

I enjoy listening to Heavy Metal, but as a child of the 60s, 70s, and to some extent the 80s, musically speaking, I am even closer to Hard Rock/Blues Rock, with the boundaries being fluid. Not least because, in my opinion, despite its many sub-genres, Heavy Metal often places more emphasis on sound than on the song itself.

You can enjoy (or not enjoy) a sound and it is to a certain extent arbitrarily, while a song burns itself into your brain and your ears and is immortalized there.

Black Hole Sun achieves this in an excellent way – it is not a headbanger, but rather a song presented at a slow pace, with the melodic beginning having little or nothing to do with Heavy Metal, until the still melodic but forceful, powerful refrain introduces Metal into the mix, alternating with quieter passages until the end.

This is not the material that Heavy Metal is made of, but rather the material from which great songs are woven and which you can listen to until our sun disappears into the black hole.

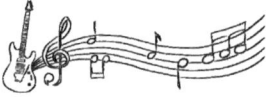

BLACK MAGIC WOMAN/GYPSY QUEEN - SANTANA

(P. Green, G. Szabo)

Zing Went The Strings Of My Heart is a song by The Move, whom I really like, but unfortunately they didn't make it into this book, and they have absolutely nothing to do with Santana. But my heart always opens up like that when I hear this man and his guitar.

Carlos Santana is a giant – not in terms of his physical stature, but in terms of his musicality, skill, and style. A reliable, indispensable icon since more than 50 years, a genius. He rarely sings, his voice is his guitar, with which he merges like no other, perhaps Jimi Hendrix came close to this intimacy. Overall, singing is rather incidental, but when it happens, it's always top-notch.

Carlos' guitar is not his instrument, it is himself and he is the guitar. His sound can be heard from thousands, "always the same" his non-fans may say, but that's precisely his trademark and if you listen closely, you'll discover new nuances over and over again.

With his Latino-Tex-Mex sound, he brought completely new soundscapes into rock music, wonderful rock and drive, wonderful melodies, percussion orgies and above all his absolutely unique, incomparable guitar.

Like all great masters, he knew and knows how to gather excellent musicians around him, who often laid the foundation for their own great careers (Neil Schon with Journey, for example, see there). The band Santana is a talent incubator like hardly any other, the list of musicians is endless and hardly any album or none (I'm not checking that now) has the same lineup.

That doesn't matter at all, Carlos and his guitar are there (or "Carlos' guitar" is there), nothing more is needed to indulge in hours of listening orgies, not without knees and hips swaying. His own or other compositions, even great standards, melt and intertwine under his fingers into a dense sound carpet that infects heart and soul. Oh Carlos, my Carlos... no, I'm not gay, and could go on for pages with this praise.

And now comes the difficult part again, the choice of a song. All of them. Done. No, unfortunately that doesn't work, that would be far, far more than a few hundred and I have to make a choice...

Samba Pa Ti or *Oye Como Va* are common knowledge, his santanized versions of *Whole Lotta Love*, *While My Guitar Gently Weeps*, *Back in Black* (a rap version (!), normally doesn't work for me at all, but with Carlos' magical fingers it works excellently)... and, and, and are pure Santana, like everything else touched by this guitar wizard.

I have to decide – and I didn't cheat, this medley of two songs is one song. The great Fleetwood Mac piece is of course santanized, in this version almost common knowledge, and establishes a great connection with the other piece, of course. And the title contains a word that applies especially to Santana: Pure Magic!

If the choice of this title seems too banal, then choose any other Santana song for yourself, no matter which one – the pure magic will remain for all eternity, the name as such is exuding it.

BRIDGE OF SIGHS - ROBIN TROWER
(Robin Trower)

Robin Trower has never been as much in the limelight as some of his peers in the "guitarero" class, even though he can certainly hold his own with them. After five albums with Procol Harum, he went his own way from a sound that was classically progressive, which wasn't really his thing, although his signature was sometimes recognizable. By the way, he only joined the group after their worldwide mega-hit *A Whiter Shade of Pale* (see separate entry).

With his first, quite successful solo albums, he created an unmistakable and captivating sound – his often slow, partly Hendrix-like guitar (always these silly comparisons...) stamped the songs with their unique mark, always played in the "power trio" format, which he mostly remained loyal to throughout his life. Fortunately, despite setbacks in his health, he is still one of the old heroes who are still alive and continue to delight us with their skills. Over the course of his long career and many great albums, he turned more towards "normal" hard/blues rock, always first-class but not always as "unmistakable" as before. Although he sometimes sings himself, he usually brings in his strong partners (such as Jack Bruce) not only for that but rather lets his guitar speak for itself in extended instrumental passages.

The **Bridge of Sighs** begins with shrill, buzzing tones, probably from a synthesizer, before his guitar and the singer's impressive vocals come in. The often-repeated riff and these floating, buzzing tones in the background create a fascinating, melancholy atmosphere, later reinforced by wind noises that seamlessly transition into the next song.

This **Bridge of Sighs** may not be everyone's cup of tea, and that's okay, but I could cross this bridge over and over again for all eternity, and to those who don't know it, I highly recommend taking that step.

CALIFORNIA DREAMIN' -
THE MAMAS AND THE PAPAS
(Phillips, Phillips)

After the first British Beat explosion, the time was ripe for softer sounds and American artists made themselves more noticeable again (Beach Boys, for example – putting aside the fundamental influence of Blues and associated Rock 'n' Roll and Soul music on British Artists and all over the world). Around the same time as *Mr. Tambourine Man* by The Byrds was created (see there), this wonderfully airy-light delicacy took a little longer to become a big hit, followed by the even bigger hit *Monday, Monday* (and some others) – this enchanting mixture of Folk, Beat and heavenly melodies conquered the world.

The Mamas and the Papas (spelled here with "The," which definitely belongs to the name) could almost be described as an early version of ABBA (what about these stupid comparisons?), although musically completely different.

Two ladies and and two gentlemen formed an excellent "vocal group," with only John Phillips also playing guitar, but they composed most of their songs themselves in various constellations, as well as for other musicians (see *San Francisco* by Scott McKenzie), with whom they also helped each other out. Barry McGuire (see *Eve of Destruction*) was also part of this circle – his early version of **California Dreamin'** was not a success. This wonderful melody simply requires heavenly angelic voices and harmonies. They were even able to stamp their mark on a Beatles song (*I Call Your Name*) with their highly individual style.

For only a few years, this quartet was a "big seller," in which they left their distinct traces.

In contrast to their cheerful, sometimes melancholic songs, their story is not very pleasant. John and Michelle Phillips divorced, the group disbanded, and solo careers of all members were only very limitedly successful, at least when it comes to music. All or nothing.

The two ladies had two other special features besides their angelic voices – "Fat Mama Cass" (Elliot) with her slightly more prominent voice knew how to flirt with her corpulence and handle it humorously, no wonder with this voice, and had a short, overall moderately successful solo career before she unfortunately died too young in London – in the same room where Keith Moon of The Who took his last breath!

That apartment was rented by Harry Nilsson, who had a huge hit with *Without You* (everyone knows it – composed by two Badfinger musicians, the first band on the Beatles' Apple label...). With a little research, you come from pillar to post or even remember some facts.

Michelle Phillips' voice was hardly inferior to Mama Cass's, but her exceptionally beautiful appearance helped her to have a quite respectable acting career, not least supported by her talent.

She is the only surviving "Mama and Papa" today. If you're ever in a bad mood... then listen to a song by Mamas and Papas (without "The" spelled out explicitly in this case) and the problem is solved.

Even a miserable *Monday, Monday* ("...every other day of the week is fine..." – their wonderful second and biggest hit) can be saved with it, but to let your soul dangle and dream not only of California, **California Dreamin'** is best, even in winter, which becomes eternal summer with it.

CHILD IN TIME - DEEP PURPLE

(Ritchie Blackmore, Ian Gillan, Roger Glover, Jon Lord, Ian Paice)

"Oh no, not again," some might think. But that may just be due to my age, perhaps *Smoke on the Water* is still more firmly stuck in the ears of many people. At the time, **Child in Time** was definitely an anthem that could not be missing from any rock party, and it is still a rock anthem for eternity today.

Starting with soft keystrokes from Jon Lord, this masterpiece builds up to Ian Gillan's piercing scream in a way that had never been heard before, leaving a breathless silence after the first listen, with a craving for repetition, and once again, and once again...

Even after the umpteenth time, this song never gets boring, presented by musicians who were among the greatest in their field. Jon Lord's classical affinity (one of the best "key ticklers" of all time) can be felt in many Deep Purple songs, without taking the upper hand (and one of the few musicians whose death brought tears to my eyes), and Ian's voice comes into its own in no environment (not even in Black Sabbath, for example) like it does in Deep Purple, where he belongs. Can anyone scream better than he does in this song?

With this almost hypnotic basic rhythm... tata-taaa, tata-taaa... played by this instrument, then by that one, then by all of them, it runs almost throughout the entire opus, interrupted only by Richie's epic, magnificent guitar solo, one of the all-time best, and finally the slowly building, mighty final chord – there won't be a dry eye if you listen to it properly, I mean really listen, and let the child penetrate your ear canals and your soul. Loosely based on *Bombay Calling* by It's A Beautiful Day, but it's not "stolen".

By the way, there's no "child in time" here. The child will just see what's going on over time...

Deep Purple has the honor of appearing twice in this book as one of only two performers in total. I actually wanted to avoid that in order to offer as wide a spectrum of artists as possible, but sometimes it can't be helped.

A song in eternal time – an eternal song in time! Carved in stone, like the fantastic cover of the album *Deep Purple In Rock*, from which Child in Time comes. Carved in stone for eternity – and the breakthrough for this pioneering group.

COAST TO COAST - DUCKS DELUXE

(Nick Garvey, Sean Tyla)

From the circle around the (unfortunately) unsuccessfully hyped Brinsley Schwarz and his group of the same name, one could describe Ducks DeLuxe as the archetype of pub rock, a style that somehow sat between two chairs and never made it big, then punk came along and had some roots in it.

Fun, rock and rock'n'roll were on the banner of all pub rockers, nomen est omen. Large halls were not their stages, but rather small pubs where sweat and beer flowed in streams. Right from the first song of the first of too few albums of the luxury ducks, you can see where it's going – a reverberating, quiet count-in, recorded as if by accident, then it rocks and rolls off, causing even the most restrained listener's limbs to twitch. A great beat, a fat rock, somewhat muffled, powerful singing, flickering guitar with a great solo, irresistible rhythm – after three beats, that made me a big fan of duck-fan for all time. That's music, that's absolutely inspiring! "All right kids, are you ready?" Absolutely, let's go!

All the other tracks of this fantastic debut album convey this feeling, which also applies to the slower songs; the shine of the duck feathers cannot be easily wiped away. Commercial success did not come, and soon the duck had laid its last egg. But from that, some very noteworthy groups emerged, such as Tyla Gang or Motors, and/or the musicians enriched other groups like Graham Parker & the Rumour.

Wow, what a heritage! Pub rock generally had the problem of not being able to convey the wet and wild atmosphere and the "live-drive" in the studio, exceptions like this confirm the rule. The other way round – strange enough the live version of this exuberant song is rather tedious and the only one that can be found online (see my Spotify playlist). You'd better buy the album anyway.

One very big exception and one of the most highly underrated albums of all time is *Ducks DeLuxe*. A guarantee as a mood-lifter.

It rocks and rolls and swings from the first to the last note, from **Coast to Coast**, with the old guitar – and in between there is eternity and the guitar-pickin' ghost (lyrics).

DEAR JEAN (I'M NERVOUS) - CITY BOY

(Lol Mason, Mike Slamer)

This British band is likely unknown to many, unfortunately, and undeservedly so. With their style of "strong melodies, clever lyrics, complex vocal arrangements, and catchy guitars," they probably were caught a little bit too much between too many stools in their time, starting in the mid-70s, to have really great success.

This characterization hits the nail on the head, and I took the liberty of taking it from the English Wikipedia page – thank you for that and all. And this characterization applies especially to **Dear Jean (I'm Nervous)**.

Fat guitars, numerous breaks, calm passages, a wonderful chorus ("Deeeeaaaaar Jeeeeaaaaan"), the aforementioned vocal arrangements – this song grabbed me from the first listen while sitting on the chair between those stools and still does. I loved flapping my arms and legs off to it (and many other songs) at the disco (I associate it especially with "The Keller" in Dortmund – not a "disco" disco, but one where the rockin' party was really going), including a massive windmill air guitar during the merciless riff/chorus, waking up from trance-like steps of the calmer passages...

City Boy is a good example of "pearls before swine" – their good albums and many great songs definitely deserved more attention. If it weren't for the issue with the stools, maybe...

Sometimes it can be too much of a good thing to sit on the right stool. It's worth exploring the many other stools.

Dear Jean* is definitely sitting on the right stool and can make me nervous and knock me off my feet forever.

---

* (The fact that my first girlfriend in London, about 10 years earlier, was also named Jean, I only realized later on and it has got nothing to do with my preference for this awesome piece of music.)

EIGHT MILES HIGH - NEIL MERRYWEATHER

(Gene Clark, Jim McGuinn, David Crosby)

Most people will associate this song with The Byrds (who also have their entry in this book, ironically not with one of the songs composed by themselves like this one) – if they know it at all, especially younger generations.

The original version by The Byrds is great, and there are numerous cover versions (many of which

I don't know, so there's catching up to do), the song itself is a legacy for eternity, which you can get closer to if you are at **Eight Miles High**.

The Canadian singer, bassist, songwriter, producer, and multi-talented artist with many albums of his own and a lot of behind-the-scenes work (see also Mama Lion) doesn't really interpret the song in a new way, but simply adds a strong, fat rock sound to the jingle-jangle sound of The Byrds, taking the miles even higher.

However, the sound is more down-to-earth, including the flanging guitar at the beginning... or is it Leslie? OK, Leslie was more commonly used for Hammond organ, but also for guitars (Wikipedia knows (almost) everything), including wah-wah guitar. But here, "flanging" is correct.

These are my eight miles for eternity, which could have been a little longer – Neil's version didn't make use of extending the original three and a half minutes to at least eight minutes (like, for example, Golden Earring did with their nearly 19-minute live version, including drum and bass solos, etc., not bad at all, but overall not as concise). Eight minutes would be the perfect length for eight miles...

EPITAPH - KING CRIMSON

(Robert Fripp, Michael Giles, Greg Lake, Ian McDonald, Peter Sinfield)

The first and eponymous album by King Crimson not only had a spectacular cover for the eyes, but also equally spectacular music for the ears. Not only the individual songs, but the entire album is a prime example of immense dynamics. Dynamics... I'm repeating myself, but gladly.

Although the most well-known song of this epochal masterpiece is probably *21st Century Schizoid Man*, for me, **Epitaph** is THE standout song for more than an eternity. Its softly floating, ethereally consuming mellotron tones (a newly introduced musical instrument at the time), paired with other uncommon instruments for rock music at that time, the rolling drums, Greg Lake's moving voice, and not least the lyrics create an unusual and captivating atmosphere that has forever entranced me.

This is a song that requires careful listening, one that you have to immerse yourself in, following every single note, every change in tempo/mood, every instrument, and every word of the lyrics. "The fate of all mankind, I see, is in the hands of fools." There is nothing to add to this eternal statement, which is more relevant than ever nowadays, and is somewhat in contrast to the melancholic and enchanting melody.

But melancholy is certainly appropriate given the state of our world.

As the saying goes, "nomen est omen" – **Epitaph** should also be played at my funeral, along with a few other songs mentioned in this book.

EVE OF DESTRUCTION - BARRY MCGUIRE
(P.F. Sloan)

A classic. A one-hit wonder (although Barry McGuire has released many albums that I don't know). Surprisingly, a global hit in the cheerful, emerging, future-oriented 60s during the dawn of the flower power era.

The accusatory, pessimistic lyrics didn't really fit these times. It wasn't a "love-heartbreak" song, but the **Eve of Destruction**, and it's as relevant today as ever, albeit with a slightly different emphasis way back then. And as long as humanity exists, it will remain like this, so definitely not for eternity and not for lang anymore...

In the 60s, people were open to all sides, and some probably recognized that this song accurately described the "eternal" problems of humanity. As an anti-war song, **Eve of Destruction** was banned by some "patriotic" US radio stations during the Vietnam War, but fortunately, it didn't harm its success and may have even brought additional publicity.

Musically, **Eve of Destruction** doesn't offer much, but it does immediately stick in your ear. The slightly raspy, compelling voice of the American bard, the underlying acoustic guitar, harmonica parts, and the rhythm reminiscent of military marching music make an irresistible mix that gives the lyrics emphasis.

For this stroke of genius, I award Barry McGuire an eternity medal. Well, half of it, the other half goes to the composer, that's only fair. He has also written many other hits for many other, far more famous artists (nothing said against Barry).

(EVERYTHING I DO) I DO IT FOR YOU - BRYAN ADAMS

(Bryan Adams, Michael Kamen, Robert John "Mutt" Lange)

The Canadian musician Bryan Adams had already had quite a few hits, especially across the pond, before achieving ultimate worldwide success with this mega hit, which became one of the best-selling singles of all time, number one in many, many countries around the globe, and to this day (2020) holds the record for the single with the most consecutive weeks (16) at the top of the UK charts!

This wonderful love ballad is simply too beautiful, beautiful, beautiful! The lyrics and melody make the heart open like a blooming flower, and like rarely any song did before, and it never wants to close again.

In a certain sense, Bryan Adams is in the same "corner" as Rod Stewart, being able to do everything from soft to heavy, and also playing excellent guitar himself, unlike Rod. Oh, these comparisons, Bryan doesn't really need them, but in some duets with Rod (and others) they complement each other in an excellent way. He can also take the attractive rasp out of his voice and add it back in portion by portion, a very special talent. A snuggle-rock singer of a special kind, sometimes spelled SNUGGLE and sometimes ROCKER, often in an incomparable combination, not just of those two, but also of rock and melody.

In addition to many unforgettable songs of his own, he proves with his album *Tracks Of My Years* (a delightful play on words, connoisseurs will know what I mean) that he can not only simply cover great songs by other artists, but also incorporate his own soul into them.

Not only, but also because *(Everything I Do) I Do It For You was* "our" song, while my best of all wives Lucy (In The Sky With Diamonds) and I wrote letters to each other around half the world (with envelope, stamp, etc. and this song on cassette), before we got to know each other and got married in "real life", this is simply a proof of love for all eternity, more beautiful and compelling as it can hardly be (if there can be at all more of that, see *I Do* by Frankie Miller).

EXCERPT FROM A TEENAGE OPERA - KEITH WEST

(Philwit, Hopkins)

The group Tomorrow was not destined for great success, although they did receive some deserved attention with their psychedelic-influenced song *My White Bicycle*, which did not become a hit.

Guitarist Steve Howe later had a successful career, primarily with the band Yes, and to a lesser extent as a solo artist. And during the flower power era, singer Keith West achieved this surprising giant hit, a typical "one-hit wonder."

The song was denied the number one spot, settling for a respectable second place, but it still justifies an eternal entry – not the place, but the song.

Beginning with a light jingling reminiscent of a fairground, a beautiful and soothing melody develops, enhanced by a "cute" children's choir, far ahead of Pink Floyd's *The Wall* – an absolute rarity at the time. The sad story of the old village grocer doesn't quite fit the wonderfully flowing, rather cheerful melody. At the time, we German music fans often understood little of the lyrics and would sing along amusedly: "Großer Jack, kleiner Jack" (meaning "Big Jack, little Jack") because "grocer" sounds like "groß(er)", which is the German word for "big", "klein(er)" means "little".

Grocer Jack, the old shopkeeper, has died (that's the only way to interpret the lyrics), and now the people wish they had treated him with more respect instead of treating his daily deliveries as mere routine. And now they stand there, weeping, at a loss...

Once heard, the children's chorus will hardly leave your mind despite the sorrowful message. The planned "Teenage Opera" (to which the partially orchestral sound would also fit), from which this wonderful song was supposed to be an "excerpt," was never realized.

Wait, that's not entirely true – I just came across the fact that there is *A Teenage Opera* soundtrack, released about 30 years later, with a collection of singles by various artists, more or less related to the theme, all composed by Mark Wirtz, including, of course, *Grocer Jack*, under the pseudonym Philwit and in this case in collaboration with Keit West, whose real name is Hopkins. I'll have to do some more research on that. You never stop learning. [I did some research/listening and was disappointed.]

And I also discovered a "version" in my archive that is counted in with "two, three, four," each with a beat underneath, before the "jingling" begins – there are some things you never know...

Perhaps this title of the hit single simply sounded more interesting than just *Grocer Jack*. And possibly, and I say this without much research and may be mistaken, this was also a catalyst for The Who's rock opera *Tommy* and inspired the aforementioned children's chorus by Pink Floyd.
Either way, the old grocer and his legacy manager, Keith West, have secured their place for eternity.

FAITH HEALER – SENSATIONAL ALEX HARVEY BAND

(Alex Harvey, Hugh McKenna)
This Scottish band never really made it big outside of Great Britain and was never a big hit maker, but they did deliver some very solid, sometimes great and diverse albums.
Situated somewhere between glam and fun/hard rock, with a slight, pre-emptive punk attitude and quirky stage outfits, the skilled musicians found themselves sitting between all stools in the 70s. Nevertheless, they had their own unique style, which paradoxically manifested itself in great diversity, but still they had this unmistakable sound.
Unfortunately, their charismatic lead singer and namesake passed away much too early in 1982, but by then the band had already disbanded.

The pulsating-pumping intro of this song lasts so long that one might think the record has a skip, with light percussion sounds in the background, until gradually some instruments start to play, including some chirping and other percussion sounds. The pulsating basic rhythm intensifies more and more, becomes a catchy riff, Alex Harvey lets his strong voice be heard, supported by choir singing, and the Scots open up in the same way without sparing fat rock.

Difficult to describe with words – but anyone who has listened to this pulse for more than 7 minutes will hardly forget it.

Even though the **Faith Healer** couldn't prevent Alex's early death, the faith in eternal good music remains. And that is what the Sensational Alex Harvey Band delivered not only, but in my opinion, especially with this song.

FATHER OF NIGHT –
MANFRED MANN'S EARTHBAND
(Bob Dylan)

A big step for Manfred Lubowitz to go to London at the young age of 21, a huge step for music history.

The jazz pianist was fed up with the apartheid system in South Africa and has since played an extremely impressive and impactful role in the music business as Manfred Mann – aside from his numerous keyboard instruments, organ, piano, various synthesizers, and especially the Minimoog and just about anything with keys. With his thick horn-rimmed glasses and never really long hair, he looked and still looks like the inconspicuous accountant next door, but is a defining personality of the beat (back then) and rock scene (today).

Manfred has always put his name in the foreground, but kept himself rather in the background. As a button pusher and puppet master behind the scenes, excellent arranger, composer, and producer, he shows the way and has the great talent of gathering excellent musicians around him and reworking not only his own but also other artists' (including "classical" composers) compositions in a completely new light or better yet sound.

The numerous hits of the group Manfred Mann are an indispensable part of the 60s. A unique phenomenon – a group with the name of an individual. "Who is Manfred Mann, that great singer?" "No, the one there in the back..." The following chapter 3, Manfred Mann's Chapter III, was too far off with its eclectic jazz-rock to reap success except for some benevolent critics. Then came the big breakthrough.

Manfred Mann's Earthband combines rock and melody in an absolutely unique way, no hard rock, no metal, no pop, yet mostly groovy and rocking and often with an incomparable "twin sound" of guitar and keyboard instruments. Smooth, precise, rocking, catchy, flowing, swinging, but not shallow or trivial – simply Manfred Mann's Earthband, with a great logo on top. The sound of the earth.

With changing lineups, but always constant within themselves (maybe someone understands what I mean), the band filled large halls and arenas at times, still tours through smaller and small venues, and still delights the large fan base. Of Manfred Mann himself, you usually only see his floppy hat, which he has been wearing for a long time and which just extends above his keyboard tower. Occasionally, he dares to come forward with his shoulder keyboard (also called "keytar," learned something new again).

The live shows are as genius as the albums, it doesn't really need to be mentioned, but I'll do it anyway for those who haven't had the pleasure yet.

Once again, the choice is not easy, many songs are so wonderfully delicious and the others still so wonderful, go down like well-salted butter, but it must be made.

And, once again, a composition by mastermind Bob Dylan, to whom I have already expressed myself several times and who is probably the composer whose works appear most frequently in this book.

Nearly 10 minutes of the finest ear candy – that's what **Father Of Night** (also called *Father Of Night, Father Of Day*) offers, starting with quiet, ethereal singing, followed by a short organ thunderstorm, then beautiful organ sound without thunder, then great vocals, keyboards in a fantastic interplay with the guitar in this typical Manfred Mann's Earthband sound, drums not to be forgotten of course.

Perfect in melody and rhythm, with strong riffs in between. Why am I talking so much, you just have to listen to it! The earth won't exist forever, but the father of night and day will have a say in eternity, I'm sure – maybe he is even eternity itself.

FLY LIKE AN EAGLE - STEVE MILLER BAND
(Miller)

Good things come to those who wait, and that is especially true for the "Stefan Müller Kapelle," as we sometimes jokingly called them as a literal German translation. Rooted in the blues and founded in San Francisco, even their early albums with their lightly psychedelic touch, relaxed swinging sound, and unusual melodies and ingredients (like a foghorn) were off the beaten path and not very successful, and hardly known in this country. Since way back when a friend put me on their trail – "no pig" knew the Steve Miller Band at that time – I have been following them (trail and band) consistently until today (which would mean my friend was a pig – which he definitely was not!).

Steve is not a big ego star, but he is the boss – the members of his band fluctuate, he calls the shots and writes most of the songs, he is an excellent guitarist, singer, and keyboardist. His songs and music are... his songs and music, not hard rock, not soft pop, but Steve Miller rock with his rather gentle, very pleasant voice, his understated guitar style without expansive solos, a strange and strangely good mixture of everything possible, including spacey interludes that Steve incorporates perfectly. A true art, to create this typical and unique sound from so many rather indifferent ingredients. Spectacular because unspectacular!

It was a slow upward climb, quality and perseverance often pay off – *The Joker* first made waves internationally, before from the mid-70s onwards, with some mega-albums, the temporary status of megastar began, filling large stadiums with ease just as his music was.

Fly Like An Eagle was the album and song that launched his great career into the air. This choice is once again a "standard" – but what makes a standard if not excellent quality and worldwide success? The eagle took off with a pinpoint landing on the elements mentioned above – as impossible as that may seem, it rises effortlessly into the air time and time again.

Who could blame Steve for "copying" this formula for some more hits and hit albums, I certainly don't, before things quieted down for him? To this day, he produces good to very good music, unfortunately nowadays more overlooked and off the mainstream, just like the early days of his career; he has his own mainstream, which is worth diving into, or maybe I should say flying into.

"Time keeps on slippin' ... into the future ..." and the future is eternity, where the eagle will forever soar.

FREE BIRD - LYNYRD SKYNYRD

(Allen Collins, Ronnie van Zant)

The debut album of these pioneering southern rockers came out of nowhere like a sparkler. The "invention of the twin-lead guitar" belongs to Wishbone Ash (most likely), but this band with the (initially) unpronounceable name (despite pronunciation instructions in the subtitle) took it up a notch with up to three lead guitars (see also Outlaws).

The album is full of strong songs, but **Free Bird** (not to be confused with the posthumous John Lennon Beatles song *Free As A Bird* with John's virtual involvement) with its more than 9 minutes of aural excitement puts the crown on the whole thing as a conclusion.

Starting with a soaring organ intro (like apparently many great songs), the wonderfully pulling-flying guitar is added soon and sets the musical theme and direction. Ronnie's strong vocals join in, followed by a return to the theme, and from around the fourth minute, **Free Bird** develops with constant tempo, and increases into an instrumental piece of the highest class.

Supported by driving drums, the guitar notes fly back and forth and/or sound in duet (or trio with flowing boundaries), "guitar frenzy" par excellence.

This **Free Bird** flies for eternity, and the album as a whole is deservedly considered one of the cornerstones and milestones of Southern rock.

I won't go into the band's tumultuous and tragic history or the often rumored origin of the name here, but I'll mention that Lynyrd Skynyrd produced many, many excellent albums until the 2010s and stayed true to their line despite numerous personnel changes, with some slight but very successful "detours" towards heavy metal.

This line also includes the fact that despite their southern behavior and image (an early marketing trick of their record company), they have no racist or right-wing intentions – this must be mentioned. Guitars and thoughts are free birds for all eternity! And, not surprisingly, the lyrics also include the line *Free As A Bird*, but the Beatles song (see above) has nothing to do with it.

FROM A DRY CAMEL - DUST
(Kerner, Wise)

What more do you need than guitar, bass, drums? Actually, nothing, except maybe a singer, and if one of these three pillars can sing, then not even that. Countless powerful "power trios" have proven this and continue to do so still today. This term was probably coined by Cream, and I won't even start listing others, as space is limited (and bands like Led Zeppelin or Black Sabbath and many others are basically "just" a power trio plus singer/shouter).

The American trio Dust released two brilliant albums in the early 70s, which are among the best that hard rock/heavy metal has to offer and still sound fresh and timeless even after fifty years. Perhaps the time was not yet ripe for them, and the remarkable cover of the first album, featuring a photo of three skeletal, real corpses from a burial chamber, may have prompted some to toss the record aside with a loud "eww." Everything turns to dust, but not these magnificent works.

Dust remained largely an insiders's tip, but the reissue of their first album on the Backbone label of my former company, Wishbone Records*, in the heavy metal-laden 80s, sold several thousand copies, showing that this tip was not quite so only an "insiders'" and that their music was and remains timeless metal dust.

Drummer Marc Bell later made a name for himself as Marc Ramone with the Ramones (rocker turns punker), and the excellent bassist Kenny Aaronson has played with everyone who's anyone in the music industry. Only the no less talented guitarist (and singer) Richie Wise soon lost interest, which is a shame.

As with many power trios, the focus is on extended instrumental passages, with the vocals serving more as decorative embellishment. Two massive gong strikes introduce **From A Dry Camel**, followed by fat drums, an equally fat bass, and another equally fat guitar with a wonderfully melodic, yet heavy riff, lightly echoed, also underscoring the vocals, before the theme continues to develop and spread, interrupted by some breaks and always accompanied by the very prominent bass, until the tempo picks up and the three musicians play their hearts out, slowing down again and then speeding up again with a guitar frenzy of the highest caliber, culminating in an overwhelming crescendo at the end. Another lesson in dynamics, melody, and pure metal.

The almost 10-minute monster opus **From A Dry Camel** is on par with other epic works like *Child In Time* by Deep Purple (see there), and as previously stated, the entire first album belongs to the crème de la crème. The second album doesn't quite measure up, but it's still well above average.

And what does the camel have to do with it? The somewhat mystical fantasy lyrics provides no clear answer. When the virgin has given her all, there is no need to be afraid, but only to let the nearby camel lie down and "go for a ride." Everyone is free to interpret this and other lyrics as they wish ("You see, there's no need to explain"); it doesn't matter. On the dust of this dried-out camel, you can ride for eternity without ever getting tired.

---

* https://de.wikipedia.org/wiki/Wishbone_Records

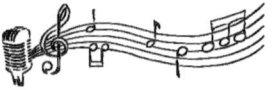

GLAD ALL OVER - THE DAVE CLARK FIVE
(Dave Clark, Mike Smith)
This ruthlessly pounding rock song with its echo sound, Mike Smith's excellent almost-shouter voice, the roaring saxophone and Dave Clark's dominant drums hit home like a bomb in 1964, soon followed by the similar *Bits & Pieces*,

announced by the previous *Do You Love Me*, which was hardly less intense.

Glad All Over displaced The Beatles' *I Want To Hold Your Hand* from the top of the UK charts, and for a short time, the Dave Clark Five were the only serious competition in the US for the rulers of the pop world there and everywhere else. This was not Mersey Beat, but hard-hitting concrete from Tottenham, London.

Dave Clark not only excelled on his drums, but he was also (and still is) absolutely exceptional as a manager and musician in personal union – and the guys, or rather Dave Clark, even owned their own large airplane! Dave Clark was as tough a businessman as his tough drums and the hard-hitting early songs – he didn't let a penny disappear into the pockets of shady managers.

Their always neat clothing and equally neat appearance contrasted with their rough, intense sound, which could later become somewhat softer and should always be paired with strong melodies, often also organ and bass-heavy, not to mention saxophone, wonderful! Perhaps even **Glad All Over** and *Bits & Pieces* deserve the honor of having invented "heavy metal", and not *You Really Got Me* by The Kinks (see there). One can argue about that, but that doesn't change the fact that this is one of the outstanding songs not only of the year but of the century.

By the way, there is a certain analogy to The Kinks – not musically – in that their second big hit (see above) was more or less a (successful) "copy" of the first. And that they too became softer over time, although no less good. By the way, the only band, as far as I know, with two different, naturally wonderful pieces of the same name – *Everybody Knows* and *Everybody Knows (I Still Love You)*. The bracket and the tracks themselves, of course, make the difference.

There were never (!) any changes in the group under this name, also very remarkable, and although they played almost exclusively original compositions, they created two medleys at a time when medleys weren't really in vogue, with *Good Old Rock'n'Roll* and *More Good Old Rock 'n' Roll*, in which they polished proven standards like *Sweet Little Sixteen, Long Tall Sally, Blue Suede Shoes, Good Golly, Miss Molly* and, and, and with their crashing steamhammer sound, also performed some other standards in full length. It doesn't get any better, if at all.

With all the great love (the Dave Clark Five ranked just behind The Beatles and Beach Boys for me at the time and are still highly, very highly regarded), I have to give a thumbs down to their film attempt *Catch Us If You Can*, even though the eponymous song and album are great – another, somewhat later hit, much less intense.

This may be because I was only able to see this work relatively recently. The Beatles' films are not a great cinematic achievement either, but they have that Beatles charm and can still be enjoyed today... and are by and with The Beatles. But if the DC5 (as they were often abbreviated) were trying to emulate that, it failed thoroughly – maybe I would have judged differently at the time (slightly), but the film was not shown in Germany (possibly for good reason).

Forget about that, the music of the Dave Clark Five is unforgettable and musically speaking/heard, it's great ear candy. Not to forget a few later tracks as Dave Clark & Friends, then also with a few other musicians.

Dave Clark is crouching like a hen on the egg over the rights and unfortunately, there are hardly any legal recordings of this great group to buy. (But, I see now, since 2019 practically all of their works are available to stream – not my thing, but if there's no other way, it's recommended to anyone.) Maybe Dave Clark wanted to top up his bulging war chest in his old age... although he should already have had enough for eternity, and he can be extremely happy and proud about that.

GOOD VIBRATIONS - BEACH BOYS
(B. Wilson, M. Love)

England was leading the way as the world's music power, until these Beach Boys from the USA arrived with their surfboards and their incomparable surf sound with wonderful castrato harmonies, a counterpoint and highly welcomed addition to British Beat dominance.

Their first huge hit, *Surfin' USA*, hinted at great things to come, even though it was "only" a version of Chuck Berry's *Sweet Little Sixteen* with different lyrics and Dick Dale's adopted surf guitar – but it was so adopted that it marked a huge milestone in the waves. Brian Wilson immediately rose to the top of the wave and set the direction, although Chuck Berry was named as the composer, anything else would have been unfair.

In the UK, people took note, but the boys quickly became part of my "Holy Trinity" at the time: Beatles-Beach Boys-Dave Clark Five, until they finally landed their first No. 1 hit in the UK with **Good Vibrations** (ironically, they had their second and last No. 1 with *Do It Again*). [Coincidentally, due to the alphabet, this entry follows that of the Dave Clark Five.]

By then, Brian had fully developed and elevated his brilliant compositional skills, often rightly celebrated as a genius. The surf sound and harmonies continued to form the basis, but he knew how to brilliantly (sigh) expand this concept. He was often compared to Lennon/McCartney, but he was only one person and he lacked the congenial partner, without wanting to diminish his great merits and abilities, I admire him.

There are many stories surrounding the legendary album *Smiley Smile*, supposedly conceived as an answer to *Sgt. Pepper's Lonely Hearts Club Band* (or just elevated to that status), which was released much, much later in its allegedly original form as *Smile*. Of course, it cannot compare to the century's work (at least) of the Beatles, but it does contain some glorious songs and those **Good Vibrations** in the typical, but brilliantly (sigh again) expanded Beach Boys sound.

Good Vibrations will continue to send the universe into **Good Vibrations** for eternity, closely followed by many other wonderful Beach Boys songs that ride on the infinite sound waves (which don't really exist in the universe, but only as transformed, oscillating radiation waves).

HALO OF FLIES - ALICE COOPER

(Alice Cooper, Neal Smith, Denis Dunaway, Michael Bruce, Glen Buxton)

Alice Cooper... Man, woman, androgynous, band or what? First and last, all of the above are correct. The unmasked, seemingly harmless band leader and solo artist with the female name Alice Cooper, son of a preacher and of course, a real name of his own, takes on the persona of a bloodthirsty vampire monster on stage, often sporting a live boa constrictor around his neck in earlier times, and combines equally bloodthirsty horror elements with, indeed, excellent music in his unique show.

Initially, he was ridiculed or scorned by many, but he rose to fame with his early hits *I'm Eighteen* and especially *School's Out*, supported by his show elements. I took note of these hits benevolently at the time; his slightly raspy voice and the mix of rock, hard rock, pop, and glamour (far ahead of its time) had something special to it, no question. I discovered the album *Killer*, which was already created before **School's Out**, coming a bit later – and it's a real killer album that blew me away and still does!

The above elements are perfectly combined in every song here, especially in **Halo Of Flies**. Sparse intro with guitar and drums, wonderfully added bass, pumping organ, a great riff, and one almost thinks it's an instrumental piece until Alice lets his pipes ring out, later making room for a short combined drum/bass solo, and the guitar doesn't fall behind either... and once again, a glorious example of the dynamic I love so much, snappy rock with a hefty dose of melody, as in all the songs by Alice Cooper (that I know). 8 minutes of listening pleasure at its finest, hardly undermatched by other songs on this masterpiece album, such as the title track or the crashing *Under My Wheels*.

Until recently, I wasn't aware that a distinction is made between the band Alice Cooper with only a few albums and the solo artist Alice Cooper with a multiple number of albums. Fortunately, the sound is always similar and always great. This also applies to later works, and if I describe the band album *Killer* as one of the best or maybe even the best under this name, it is as always my personal opinion but should be reagarded with particular caution in this case – I don't know most of the albums. Again, a gap that needs filling.

As was usual in the past, one often only understood half or nothing of the lyrics (see book reference under *Child In Time*), and for a while, I thought the title might have something to do with the book "Lord of the Flies", but it does not. Rather, the halo of flies is a metaphor for death and fits well with the lyrics, which, like everything interpreted by Alice Cooper, have a slight but intense sense of irony.

Wow, this article has become much longer than anticipated, but that doesn't matter. Alice Cooper deserves it, as a pioneer and trendsetter for over-the-top stage shows (Kiss, Iron Maiden, and others) and as a show talent in the best sense, with great music. With over 50 years in the business, one can only hope that his personal **Halo of Flies** is still a long way off – may these flies last for eternity.

HANDLE WITH CARE -
TRAVELING WILBURYS

(Traveling Wilburys)

If there could only be one group labeled "Supergroup," it would be this one. Even a mega-supergroup.

Huh? All five musicians are named (or rather call themselves) Wilbury, with the first names Otis, Nelson, Charlie T., Lefty, and Lucky. And what's so "super" about that? Five mega-stars wanted to break free from their status and just do what they enjoyed. George Harrison, Roy Orbison, Bob Dylan, Tom Petty, Geoff Lynne – these names take some getting used to, and of course, it was an open secret that was already revealed through the album cover's pictures, even though these names were never officially mentioned anywhere.

Supported by notable other musicians and a charming (fictional) story about the origin of the Wilbury clan... If I were to go into each of these musicians individually, it would exceed the scope. The readers know (or should know) about it. A quickly fading shooting star in the pop/rock sky – **Handle With Care** was a hit, as was the album, and that was pretty much it, unfortunately. Roy Orbison passed away, leaving only four, and they made a second album titled Vol. 3 – I love these little games.

Both albums were only available for a short time. George had the rights and didn't want to reissue the works, for whatever reason. On the second album, the four remaining Wilburys had different first names again... There are many stories about it, and George's son Dani is involved in the background as "Ayrton Wilbury," in honor of the racing driver Ayrton Senna, and Gary Moore also makes an appearance as "Ken Wilbury." At live events, there can sometimes be a gathering of such mega-stars, but not so much in the studio.

Spectacular "real" names – not so spectacular music, but with their relaxed, wonderfully swinging mix of rock and folk music, they leave a distinct mark with the desire for more and more Wilburys, a first-rate sense of well-being. You don't have to handle it with care, and even Bob Dylan's limited singing skills come to the fore here, not to mention Roy's wonderfully melting, powerful voice, etc. (his "Pretty Woman" also deserves a mention, like some other songs, but... 100 is 100, no strings attached, sigh).

Even though the shooting star faded quickly, it keeps reappearing, and the Wilburys may travel on it into eternity.

HEARTLESS WORLD - TEAZE
(M. Bradac, M. Kozak)
Canadian rockers Teaze haven't left a big impression in the annals of rock history and are hardly known even in their home country.

In that regard, they share the fate of many artists, despite their solid work. Solid work in terms of both musical ability and songwriting skills.

One result of their solid, and in this case, more than solid work is this song, which, in my opinion, leaves a great impression and clearly qualifies for this collection. Initially, there's a relaxed, melodic guitar playing and excellent vocals, which are interrupted by a break, resumed, interrupted again, and then escalate with a heavy riff. A solo that sounds similar to a brass instrument, but probably comes from a Moog synthesizer, and again, that beautiful melody – a fat riff, followed by strong vocals, the singer's ecstatic screams, and the ever-evolving melody. Simply beautiful, I must say again, but also groovy and more pomp rock than hard rock, yet with strong roots, it packs a punch! The outstanding singer doesn't make you miss a genuine guitar solo.

Nomen est omen – a world that lets a song of such quality disappear into obscurity is truly heartless. This has been one of my favorites for a long time, and I've just now become aware that apparently I'm not the only one who likes it: it has been used as a soundtrack for two movies, one of which is a horror anthology. I don't quite understand that, perhaps it's because of those screams – but **Heartless World** is absolutely not horror, but an eternally delightful listening pleasure that no one should miss out on.

HIGHWAY TO HELL - AC⚡DC

(Young, Young & Scott)

To hell with it, with this selection of good, great, excellent, outstanding, and overwhelming songs, I'm sweating like being in hell itself (probably, I haven't been there personally, yet).

I admit – when I first heard these Australian (back then) young dudes, I smirked condescendingly, but already the second alternating current/direct current electrocution totally electrified me, not just because of their cool logo. [The only band for which I even attempted to replicate the logo, at least somewhat.]

Rock, hard rock taken to the ultimate point – inexplicably the same, yet always different riffs that make electric high voltage feel like a mild tingle, crisp solos, and that voice, which you could hear all the way from Australia to here, even without a mic. Even though it was later seamlessly "thanks" to tragic circumstances replaced by an English tube of the same caliber, "replacement" doesn't sound right.

AC⚡DC are special in every way, starting, of course, with their excellent music, from Angus' guitar whiz in his short-pants schoolboy uniform to the two successive and incomparable singing/screaming voices, and the band's talent to create something new out of the "same old sound" (as their foolish opponents say) over and over again. Once AC⚡DC, always AC⚡DC – if there were a band you had to invent if it didn't exist, it'd be this one!

I was lucky to see/hear them live with both Bon and Brian, some of the unforgettable experiences among hundreds, if not thousands, of concerts. Once AC⚡DC, always AC⚡DC! I dare say no other group has served hard rock better than them.

And now comes the agony of choice... of course, **Highway to Hell** is a typical banger, just like almost every other of their pieces, but perhaps a bit more emphatic, with a particularly catchy chorus, and the title speaks for itself. The **Highway to Hell** – my favorite football (yes, it's the real football, ignorants call it soccer) club, VfL Bochum, can truly sing a song about that, and so this song is always played in our stadium.

One more good reason to choose it here as a representative for all the wonderful AC⚡DC songs. The **Highway to Hell** leads straight to eternity, no turning back, whether it's alternating current or direct current, doesn't matter – once AC⚡DC, always AC⚡DC!

HIPPY HIPPY SHAKE –
THE SWINGING BLUE JEANS
(Chan Romero)

As a perfect synthesis of rock 'n' roll and beat, this song somehow ushered in a new era at the end of

1963. The relatively and at the time certainly "heavy" guitar sound, especially the shout-singing, and that short "primitive scream" before the brief, distinctive, and remarkable guitar solo were unheard of back then, haha – that was this "Negro music" that our parents tried to warn us about (fortunately not mine – though not necessarily welcomed, it was tolerated, for which I am very grateful).

The Beatles also had this song in their early repertoire, even before the Swinging Blue Jeans. But, at least as it is preserved on recordings, not as impressive as the Swinging Blue Jeans. Almost sacrilegious to write this, but the "gods" Beatles were at that time just four Liverpool boys, seeking their path... and finding it.

After a little over a minute and a half, the fun is over, but those minutes pack a punch!

The Swinging Blue Jeans incorporated many rock 'n' roll standards that one can listen to and should (*Long Tall Sally, Tutti Frutti*, and, and, and – their version of *Shakin' All Over* or especially *Good Golly, Miss Molly* is also very noteworthy). However, they more or less disappeared amidst the throng of beat groups, despite hailing from Liverpool and mastering the Mersey Beat well, but ultimately not significantly enough. (They continue to tour to this day with multiple lineup changes.)

They could sing and sound well, their second big hit *You're No Good* in a pleasing Mersey Beat sound gave hope once more, but they could never reach the high bar set by **Hippy Hippy Shake** to stand out from their fellow competitors. They might have done more with the distinctive, somewhat rough scream voice of their lead singer. The blue jeans swung only for a brief moment – but they left an impressive footprint for eternity.

HOUND DOG - ELVIS PRESLEY
(Leiber, Stoller)

Of course, the "King" must not be missing, but that's how quite some musicians are referred to (or refer to themselves). But if there's one, there's only one – Elvis!

Still, this book is primarily about songs, and this Rock 'n' Roll classic is, in my opinion, particularly impressive in Elvis's version.

The **Hound Dog** allows for many interpretations, and the "Gigolo" interpretation is probably the most fitting. And the rabbits he doesn't catch... there were those Bunnies... everyone can make their own guess about that.

Not written especially for him, but the way Elvis personifies and brilliantly interprets this song, it seems like tailor-made for him, and many (like myself) will associate this song with the "King" and remember him with this song. At this point, let's also take a moment to appreciate the artists who are rarely in the spotlight but without whom all these wonderful songs wouldn't exist – the composers.

The duo Leiber/Stoller is responsible for what feels like half of all the hits of the later 50s and early 60s, and they cannot be praised highly enough. Only Lennon/McCartney and perhaps Jagger/Richards, later also Elton John and a few others, received great public attention as composers. It is often overlooked that a "good song" requires two elements – the composition as the foundation and the performer who brings it to life and takes the spotlight.

Fortunately, the contractual side is usually arranged in a way that composers get their fair share of the cake – if I'm not mistaken, and sometimes even more than the performers. I'm not an expert in this field. I was never a huge Elvis fan; after my "big bang" (The Beatles), I initially saw him as a "dated corny guy" – may he forgive me – and only later came to appreciate him; his early death unexpectedly touched me considerably back then.

Elvis himself could be a perfect gigolo with his charisma, his expressions (where did Billy Idol get his sneering lip from?), and the "provocative" hip swaying ("Elvis the pelvis"), which garnered the enthusiasm of countless female fans and the (secret) admiration of males and the wrath of prudish white WASP (White Anglo-Saxon

Protestants) society. Well done, Elvis – you were and will forever be a true great!

He played a significant role in the development of Rock 'n' Roll, had excellent musicians and managers around him, and gave this and other songs (like *Jailhouse Rock*) his unique style – the wild, untamed Elvis of the earlier years was the best!

I've chosen the songs in this book based on my taste, I already mentioned that, and sometimes I later researched about them, which brought some surprises. For instance, **Hound Dog** was ranked 19th in the Rolling Stone music magazine's list of the 500 greatest songs of all time in 2004 (ultimately just the taste of competent music journalists but still noteworthy). Leiber and Stoller were ranked 20th in the same magazine's list of the greatest composers of all time in 2015, and their autobiography is titled... **Hound Dog**. Fits perfectly!

HOUSE OF THE RISING SUN - THE ANIMALS

(Traditional)

Oh no, not this campfire stuff again, some of you might groan. BUT! Exactly. Even though The Animals had many other unforgettable hits, this track is special – not just because it was their first big hit (No. 1 in the UK and USA).

Contrary to the trend of that time, guitars are not the focus (except for the intro), but the Hammond organ, which became popular with it; the amazing organ of the young Eric Burdon – that's talking about his voice – gives this "Traditional" a very special touch. This wonderful song also introduced us Beat enthusiasts to the blues, without which there would be no Rock 'n' Roll or Beat, etc.

Played and listened to endlessly over and over again, this version is considered by many as the "Original" – which doesn't actually exist, as this song is truly "traditional", at that time already decades old and more, and no composer is known.

The Animals imprinted their timeless stamp on this incomparable song with their earthy, distinctive sound and, so to speak, created this "Original". Also highly recommended is the rock version by Frijid Pink, who scored a big hit with it 6 years after The Animals, their only one. That once again speaks to the quality of the song itself.

Not just because of Eric Burdon with his long, eventful career, The Animals were a big deal – organist Alan Price later scored some great hits with his band Alan Price Set, and bassist Chas Chandler, as the "discoverer" and first manager of Jimi Hendrix, wrote a very special chapter in music history.

If there's any house standing in eternity at all, it would be that of the rising sun.

(I CAN'T GET NO) SATISFACTION - THE ROLLING STONES

(Jagger, Richards)

Of course, this catchy tune and this band must not be missing here. But this piece is more than just a catchy tune.

The Beatles set the stone rolling for the greatest music and cultural revolution of the 20th century by taking the small rock 'n' roll pebble from across the pond, adding a few other ingredients, and above all, bringing themselves in with their extraordinary talent and unique magic.

This revolution happened elegantly and, so to speak, unnoticed, as the Beatles quickly became popular "common property," at least in England, soon everywhere in the world. They were neat, nice, and responsible for countless tears and wet panties among the female population. That doesn't mean they were a "girl band." On the contrary, they were THE super band, music gods – enough has been said about this and their constantly groundbreaking influence and innovations, not least in my book...*

The Rolling Stones were cut from a different cloth, rough, rebellious (outwardly), and they

Ferdinand Köther

gratefully embraced the rolling stone, but the Beatles had already rolled it further. They had their fair share of female fans too, but they were more hated by the older generation, making them more attractive to self-proclaimed or perceived "underdogs."

From the beginning, a large part of the Beatles' recordings consisted of their own compositions, and pretty soon, it was almost exclusively their own work. The Rolling Stones, on the other hand, relied on cover versions for a long time, skillfully bending them in their distinctive direction. Their second somewhat bigger hit was *I Wanna Be Your Man* – a Lennon/McCartney composition, and it took some time for Jagger and Richards to discover their own talent. Their first "original" big hit was *The Last Time* (ironically named), followed by this excellent anthem (and many other great Jagger/Richards songs) of rebellion and youth discontent, asserting their own rights and demanding attention. It's not about the lack of "satisfaction" in picking up a girl (well, a little bit at the end of the song), but about the rebellious outcry that has been resonating through the decades with this musical statement. The Beatles paved the way, the Rolling Stones and others cleared the path afterward...

I don't want to delve into the alleged rivalry between the Beatles and the Stones or fuel it; they were friends and appreciated each other. There can be no rivalry between two completely different entities.

"I want more, this is not enough for me" is a rough interpretation (or better adaptation) in the sense of the song, which, with its brilliant riff, is both a milestone and a monument for the Rolling Stones, who are still rolling on. Probably not forever, unfortunately, but this masterpiece will definitely endure for eternity and is one of those pieces that everyone truly knows, unless they come from another planet.

* Ferdinand Köther: Ich glaube an Hühner / BoD,
ISBN 978-3-739206356

I DO - FRANKIE MILLER
(Francis J. Miller)

Frankie...who? That's what some people might say if they don't know this gifted singer. His fantastic albums, mostly from the 70s, offer a wonderful mix of pub-rock, R 'n' B, and a touch of soul, owed especially to his slightly rough, wonderfully powerful voice, with which he knows (or knew) how to handle the best. His music immediately gets into your blood and makes you want to dance, but unfortunately, he never achieved major breakthrough success. At least he landed a Top Ten hit in the UK with *Darlin'* in 1978.

A serious illness put an end to his career in the 90s; he couldn't perform anymore and, at times, couldn't even speak (let alone sing, of course). Later, he was able to record some demos again.

These demos, remastered and refined with the support of many friends, can be found on the great album *Double Take* (2016) – a title with multiple meanings, as almost all recordings are duets with other singers/artists, with Frankie (almost) always leading the way. The list of friends includes Joe Walsh, Rod Stewart, Elton John, Bonnie Tyler, and many more.

Now I've written a lot about the context, but nothing about this song. **I Do** is one of the most beautiful and heartfelt love ballads I've ever heard, and it's the only song on this album that is solely attributed to Frankie, not a duet.

Sparingly instrumented, his already slightly fragile voice must touch every heart to its deepest core and for all eternity with this sincere and convincingly performed declaration of love – if it doesn't do that, one should question if they have a heart.

Rod Stewart once said that Frankie is the only white singer who has ever brought tears to his eyes. Nothing can be added to that.

It's only to be hoped that there are more demos like this, or that Frankie will still be able to create such recordings. I hope so very much – **I do**!

I DON'T WANT TO MISS A THING - AEROSMITH

(Diane Warren)

"Der Luftschmitz," as us German guys used to call this band, possibly even somewhat disdainfully and considering their significance in the rock business unjustified. I can't even remember if I paid attention to their first two albums at all. The third one, *Toys In The Attic*, completely convinced me (and still does). After that, I somehow lost track of the "Luftschmiede" (sounds a bit less derogatory), except for occasional catchy hits.

That might be because they are a "typical American band," hugely successful in the US but less present here, both on concert stages and in the charts (that changed only in and after the '90s). No American hard rock band has sold more albums than them! A big draw on stadium stages, their hard rock is a mix of just that, some metal, pop, and occasional blues elements. Sometimes, for my taste, it's a bit too uniform and smooth, but I'm flexible and open to learning, and I'm starting to rediscover them more now. These guys forge much more than just hot air. It's not unlikely that they will eventually become part of my "complete collection obsession"; you're never "done" until your last breath...

The parallels to the by now longest-serving band in the world are coincidental but still remarkable. It starts with a certain resemblance between Steven Tyler and Mick Jagger, although Jagger's "pout" is a cute little kissy mouth compared to Tyler's. The singer and guitarist (Perry and Richards, respectively) form a brilliant songwriting duo and are responsible for most of the songs. The lineup has been practically constant for about 60 and 50 years (even more constant than the Rolling Stones'), and the memorable logo has remained almost unchanged – both of them being among the greatest acts of all time.

The Stones are more raw, and their music is completely different, but Steven Tyler can sing better. Even if the Stones' fans might want to stone me for this, it doesn't matter – I mean "sing"; Mick Jagger doesn't need to sing, he's Mick Jagger, has his voice, and that's enough!

Enough of the silly comparisons. Steven Tyler, with his pleasantly slightly raspy voice, belongs to the class of "cuddly rockers" like Rod Stewart or Bryan Adams (sorry, comparisons again – no, references). And when his voice is presented so excellently and distinctively with the crisp, melodic riffs and solos of Joe Perry (and Brad Whitford), it's often a special listening pleasure that might leave the hardcore rocker as undecided as the soft pop fan.

How excellently and uniquely Tyler can sing is demonstrated once again in this wonderful ballad, a beautiful love song and a real tear-jerker. Originally "just" a song for a movie, **I Don't Want To Miss A Thing** became their biggest worldwide hit, atypically not composed by Tyler/Perry, who can write beautiful ballads in addition to rocking tunes. Aerosmith contributed three more songs to the movie *Armageddon* (in which Tyler's exceptionally pretty daughter Liv also appears – known at the latest from *Lord of the Rings*, among others), but none of them touch the heart like this one. I should watch the movie sometime.

The piece starts like a boring, even extremely boring piece of so-called "classical" music (probably in tribute to its status as a "soundtrack"), and you might feel like turning it off, but then, just in time, comes Steven's tender crooning, accompanied initially by sparse instrumentation. It gradually builds up, and a magnificent rock ballad unfolds, not only showcasing Steven's singing in a special way but also proving that hardly anyone can scream so beautifully shrill and melodic to the point where it breaks your heart.

I don't want to miss this song for eternity, and may the "Luftschmiede" keep flying and forging forever.

IMAGINE - JOHN LENNON

(John Lennon, Yoko Ono)*

Ah, so some might think, the Beatles after all – no, John Lennon was a Beatle, one of four, perhaps one of the most important (if you can even say that), but that's not up for debate here.

John Lennon was one of the most influential figures of possibly the penultimate century of humanity, not only as a Beatle or ex-Beatle. His artistic abilities beyond the world of music and politically driven activities deserve the highest respect – and this song deserves the highest of all! One of the most covered and played songs, John's original is light-years ahead of all other attempts.

Gentle piano playing and John's unmistakable voice seem to lull the listener, but those who listen closely will quickly awaken again. The problems of our world could not be described better, even if the environmental aspect wasn't as prominent or conscious back then.

The melody is enchanting, the lyrics valid for millennia, and even in the future, if there is one – probably not, though. But this song will endure for all eternity. To write much more about it would be prohibited by respect and admiration and would be utterly unnecessary anyway.

Imagine... an island and only one song you could take along, it would probably have to be this one. "You may say I'm a dreamer..."

* *Note:* **Imagine** was long considered a composition by John Lennon; it wasn't until 2017 that Yoko Ono was granted the right as a co-author.

I'M A MAN -
CHICAGO TRANSIT AUTHORITY

(Stevie Winwood/James Miller)

Chicago, the band, not the city – a multifaceted conglomerate of skilled musicians, probably known here in Europe more for their wonderful ballads, if at all (still).

Their often dominant, skillful "brass" isn't quite my thing, but they could also get "seriously intense," especially in the beginning when they were still called Chicago Transit Authority. The name changed with their second album to Chicago, and this "brass ensemble," hailing from Chicago, naturally, and usually comprising at least 7 members (often more), from the get-go brought the full throttle with the motto "go big or go home": Mostly double albums or even more, mostly just sequentially numbered – exceptions for both cases confirm the rule. Especially in the USA, Chicago were a big deal for years, and they're among the bands with the best-selling albums of all time worldwide.

Rarely do I value cover versions higher than the original – especially when, as in this case, the original by the Spencer Davis Group (see there) is a powerhouse piece that would also deserve this entry.

However, Chicago Transit Authority manages to transform this powerhouse piece into something different, something new – not just covering it, but interpreting it. Starting with a delightful bass line, then the drums kicking in, and castanet-like percussive sounds sneaking in, followed by an earthy organ sound, before Terry Kath's guitar breaks through with an unparalleled sound – sound, sound, sound, paired with a strong song, that's precisely it. The good vocals (including Terry Kath's) don't bother me, I'll just leave it at that.

A break, percussion, organ, that pulling, probing guitar again, the chorus – you can bask in this song and sound for well over 5 minutes, before it fades out with almost experimental guitar acrobatics.

Terry Kath goes to the extreme with guitar acrobatics in *Free Form Guitar*, and I don't blame anyone for covering their ears or tuning out. I can't get enough of it.

But Chicago Transit Authority, or rather Chicago by then, couldn't earn enough dollars from it (no blame).

Personally, I would have preferred if Chicago had continued down this hard path; at the latest with Terry Kath's death in 1978, the transit train veered into significantly more commercial territory (still no blame) with equally successful outcomes.

IN-A-GADDA-DA-VIDA – IRON BUTTERFLY

(Doug Ingle)

If ever a group was/will be identified with just one song, then we have the precedent here. Legends surround the name of this song on their second album of the same name, most of which boil down to it not meaning anything and simply being "nonsense" lyrics that fit well with the song's rhythm.

Back then, albums still had two sides, but hardly anyone listened to the first side of this one, or at all. The second side was played until it was scratched and worn out – it consisted of 17 minutes of **In-A-Gadda-Da-Vida**. No hippie party or any other event without this hypnotic song, well into the 70s. The shrunken two-and-a-half-minute single version was a hit – the album too, of course – but no comparison to the "real" piece.

Gentle and soft organ intro, then bass, drums, and the heavy guitar riff that almost continuously leaves its mark, vocals that soon fade away and make room for extended solos – drums, organ, bass, guitar with distortions and unusual tones for the time. Very repetitive, this work ingrains itself indelibly in your ears, trance-like, and probably many a trip was underscored with this music in the background.

Aside from the nonsense title and a few more lines, **In-A-Gadda-Da-Vida** is practically an instrumental piece that impressively combines psychedelic and prefigured heavy metal effects. In the same year, Cream also released *Wheels Of Fire* with an even more extended drum solo, that was the trend of the time, but possibly one of these albums was the first with this feature – I'm not researching that now, perhaps a reader/listener knows more about it and can let me know.

The band could never replicate this fantastic stroke of genius, but it's also entirely sufficient to secure them a guaranteed place for eternity.

As I'm only finding out now (once again thanks to Wikipedia), Iron Butterfly has existed with interruptions and an incredibly high number of lineup changes up until today, with their last few albums released in 1975! Only the drummer remains from the original days, though not from the very first day and also with interruptions. Did I miss something? If I did, that's life (one of the possible interpretations of the title in short form) – In-All-Goodness-Definitely-Vibrant!

IN THE YEAR 2525 - ZAGER & EVANS
(Rick Evans)

There are about a handful of "one-hit wonders" in this book (I'm not counting them right now), also known as "one-day flies," and this opus is one of them. This is not meant disrespectfully, but these artists are distinguished by having a huge hit and then quietly fading into obscurity – not to be taken literally, because they all sang and played on for a while longer, without further success.

The American pop-folk-rock duo known as Zager & Evans, consisting of Denny Zager and Rick Evans, had a dream start with this song – so dreamy that it was over just as quickly, not unlike their wonderful song itself when you listen to the lyrics.

The soothing melody and strong vocals, backed by a good beat and swinging folk guitars, sound almost cheerful, but the lyrics are anything but that. Musically fitting the fading Flower Power era, Rick Evans shows incredible foresight for the year 1969.

Starting in the year 2525, "if man is still alive", it continues at intervals of 1010 years until 6565 with shocking visions that have already partially come true by now or been surpassed.

Then the mood changes, also musically (has something to do with changes in the minor key, I'm not a musician – aside from being a bad drummer – and notes are a mystery to me), and it continues with 7510, 8510, and finally 9595.

By then, humanity has " … taken everything this old earth can give, and he ain't put back nothing."

In the year 10,000, humanity has finally become extinct. That's optimistic again because I'm sure that this germ called "Man" won't even make it to the year 2525.

Perhaps the listeners were and are simply captivated by the wonderful melody without really listening or realizing what was subtly slipped to them without pointing fingers, or maybe they just thought, "*Oh, well* ..." (Not that Fleetwood Mac song, see there.) In 1969, the world still looked pretty rosy.

The end of the world was probably never described more beautifully, but, O*h well*, this won't be the end of the world, but only the decline of the dumbest species that has inhabited (and destroyed) this planet so far. A "one-hit wonder" indeed, just not as successful as this magnificent song.

In eternity, **In The Year 2525** will continue to resonate forever, "… but through eternal night, the twinkling of starlight …"

But until eternity arrives, nature probably has a few more opportunities to correct its first mistake, to create intelligent beings. But maybe I'm doing some animal species injustice with that statement and should rather say beings who use their intelligence better than to destroy themselves and their own world. On many other of the billions (the actual number is hardly expressible) of planets in the universe, there will certainly be such beings (and probably many as foolish as here), why not also in the future on this one, just for a change?

I SEE NO REASON - TITANIC
(Robinson, Aas)

We haven't exactly been flooded here in our country with pop or rock from Norway, apart from the formidable a-ha in the '80s and even later. Oh, Wencke Myhre was also from Norway, not my music, but cute and in her own way, a big star. And Maria Mena ... and many more, in Norway.

Maybe some readers still remember Titanic, who in the early '70s (exactly 1970) scored a fantastic instrumental hit with *Sultana* (not dissimilar to the Santana sound, maybe that's why the name?).

But on their first album, there was an even "classier" song (*Sultana* was on their second album). **I See No Reason** is not only "classier" but powerful and overwhelming. To the fantastic sound of the roaring church organ, reminiscent of Procol Harum's greatest hit, strong, melancholic and emotional vocals soon join in, a background choir is added, building-up slowly... oh yeah, the dynamics that have always fascinated me, constantly accompanied by this wonderful organ sound. A break, only drums, organ – and again, because it's so beautiful, with slightly different lyrics... break, only drums, organ, then only drums for a long time, with a simple beat... followed by a long, magnificent guitar solo... and that organ, did I mention it... the returning vocals, a break, only drums again, choir, culminating in a chilling scream at the end, worthy of Deep Purple.

Even though other bands had to serve as a comparison here, Titanic have their absolutely unique sound, without copying. Overall, across all their albums, they offer top-notch pop-rock, and **I See No Reason** is a top-class rock ballad that you can indulge in for more than 8 minutes.

I see no reason why this masterpiece shouldn't qualify for eternity – it was one of the first on my mental list for this book. However, why the band recorded a new version in the 2000s is a mystery to me. It's not bad listening to it, but there's no comparison to the original recording So, for anyone who should embark on the search for it – be warned.

And by the way, apart from Norway, if you like melodic heavy metal, you should check out Audrey Horne. No, that's not a singer but a recommendable metal band from the North, with some very slight hints of Wishbone Ash – why am

I talking like this and why do I always have to make comparisons when it comes to Norwegian bands? Silly.

The RMS Titanic may have sunk, but Titanic will forever ride on top of the waves of my "Top 100" with this excellent song.

I SEE THE RAIN - MARMALADE

(William Junior Campbell, Dean Ford)

This "best hit that never was," as I like to say, definitely belongs to the 100 songs for eternity, at least for me.

Starting with thunder, rain, and an irresistible guitar hook that runs throughout the whole song and is an earworm like no other, this sound echoed from all corners of London and its surroundings in 1967, which surprisingly did not lead to a chart placement, unlike the later, mostly softer big pop hits of this Scottish group, initially written with "The" (which would be correct here), later without. Their cover version of the Beatles' song *Ob-La-Di, Ob-La-Da* (from the brilliant *White Album* of the Fab Four – brilliant like all their works, perhaps a tiny bit less than their masterpiece *Sgt. Pepper's Lonely Hearts Club Band*) was their biggest hit, reaching No. 1!

Equally surprisingly, the later well-established pop vocals (here with some assistance from Graham Nash of the Hollies) fit perfectly with the progressive "heavy" sound, far ahead of its time.

I See The Rain exudes a Hendrix feeling, and practically simultaneously, Jimi Hendrix released *Hey Joe* and it became a big hit – which makes you wonder why this outstanding song didn't. One of the first and few songs, or perhaps the first (?), with environmental sounds.

By the way, Marmalade also covered *Hey Joe*, not bad at all, but of course, no comparison to Jimi's version of this "traditional." But what greater praise is there than the fact that possibly the greatest guitarist of all time, Jimi Hendrix himself, described **I See The Rain** as one of his favorite songs of 1967? This proved that he was not only a master of the six strings but also had excellent taste in music.

The success that **I See The Rain** truly deserved, as mentioned earlier, came later with "poppy," always good and catchy songs, which somewhat reconciled me. I don't eat marmalade, but I love Marmalade!

At the Woburn Abbey Festival of the Flower Children*, I had the chance to experience **I See The Rain** live, among other songs – there was a bit of rain too, yes, but above all, the song, presented by the artists themselves.

---

* http://www.ukrockfestivals.com/woburn-67.html

(I also contributed a little to this website: a few photos (not of Marmalade) and some text, translated from my German autobiography.

These photos can also be found in the beautiful picture book with little accompanying text by Sam Knee: "Memory of a Free Festival – The Golden Era of the British Underground Festival" / Cicada Books Limited, ISBN 978-1-908714435. Although Woburn Abbey was not a "free" festival.)

ITCHYCOO PARK - SMALL FACES

(Marriott, Lane)

Small faces they had, unsung heroes of the 1960s they still are. These London lads were never really huge stars, but they secured a solid place in music history with their fantastic hits and beyond those.

Four faces with many facets in their songs, from the raw R&B sound with Steve Marriott's soulful, distinctive voice in their early days to very relaxed, cheerful songs during the Flower Power era. Always with drive, melody, and the organ sound as a constant element – many small masterpieces that all have more or less eternal value.

Unfortunately, their career was relatively short, and their subsequent solo careers were not particularly successful. Rod Stewart and Ronnie Wood joined the three remaining Faces, and they were no longer "Small," while Steve Marriott joined Humble Pie (with Peter Frampton). For

Rod, it was a cornerstone of his mega career, while Humble Pie remained somewhat more modest but highly esteemed by devoted fans.

Their later, brief reunion went largely unnoticed. As a later, temporary "rental drummer" for The Who, with a certain affinity for their music, Kenney Jones perhaps achieved the most success outside of the original Faces.

With **Itchycoo Park**, we have the gentler, "psychedelic" sound of the great little quartet, a perfect Flower Power song that showcases the softer side of Steve's voice. A special touch is the "flanging," a unique effect similar to "phasing," which created that "psychedelic" drum sound – floating, laid-back, delightful for letting your soul wander.

Similarly laid-back is one of their other big hits, *Lazy Sunday*, which goes in the same direction without "flanging." The Small Faces could not only rock out but also write and play very beautiful, relaxed musical compositions.

There are several similar stories about the origin of the song's name. The guys liked to visit many of London's beautiful parks, especially one in particular, which had prickly plants and various insects. And then, afterward, you might get an itch...

If you're looking for **Itchycoo Park** in London, you'll search in vain, but in eternity, you'll find it effortlessly.

IT'S ABOUT PRIDE - OUTLAWS
(H. Paul)

Their debut album was (and still is) a revelation, and the same goes for almost every one of their relatively few works over the decades, which nevertheless makes it difficult to choose a song from this incredible group.

While Wishbone Ash are considered the inventors of the "twin-guitar sound," the Outlaws take it a step further, adding a third guitar for a "triplet-guitar sound" – not always, but frequently, with often just two guitars in action. And if Lynyrd Skynyrd is recognized as epigones of Southern Rock (also with 2 or 3 guitars), then neglecting the Outlaws is a grave oversight.

While the former tend to lean toward the harder side, especially on some of their later albums, the Outlaws have a slight inclination towards country, without losing their edge. Their harmonious, melodious singing is reminiscent of the Eagles or the Byrds at times. Comparisons, comparisons – the Outlaws absolutely don't need them; their unmistakable sound with this unusual combination of harmony vocals and guitar wizardry is their unique trademark. Unfortunately, they are not quite as well-known as some of the other bands mentioned, which is why these hints come with the urgent recommendation to also turn your attention to the Outlaws.

If you love guitars, you can't overlook these heroes. It's a whirlwind, buzzing, and swinging in glorious, almost indecent orgies, ranging from relaxed to heavy, and the wonderful singing rounds it all off. The perfect blend of melody, rhythm, and rock with a touch of country now and then is even more astonishing considering the immense number of lineup changes, with a few constants over longer periods, which is not noticeable/audible. The high quality has never (!) waned. Even the slightly weaker Outlaws songs – yes, they exist – are still much better than some "good" songs by other bands. The torch, in other words, the guitar and the microphone, was evidently only passed on to talents who had/have the Outlaw in their blood. Bass and drums also play no small role. Once you've heard them – an Outlaw forever!

My enthusiasm knows hardly any bounds... which song should it be now? I can't take all their fantastic songs, even though I'd love to. Perhaps the more than 8-minute orgy (I can only repeat myself), *Green Grass & High Tides* from their debut album, or *(Ghost) Riders In The Sky* from a later one... what am I saying, these are all ear-guitar-orgies that make your blood surge through the body like melted butter through a sieve. Guitars, guitars, guitars, and a great logo with the buffalo skull that has solidified over the years.

No, it shall be **It's About Pride** (or maybe *Trail of Tears*, or... oh, it's so beautifully difficult) from their comeback album of the same name released in the early 2000s (an "album of the century"). The track once again combines all their qualities perfectly, starting slow and mellow, beautiful melody, slightly country-style singing, added harmonies, the buildup with guitars, guitars, guitars... Almost every song on this fantastic, great, amazing album – I can't mention it often enough – ends in relentless guitar orgies.

Pistols and rifles are powerless against the guitar front of these outlaws who have written their own law for Southern Rock and can be proud to swing their guitars into eternity. This eternal law is engraved with and in guitars.

(Right now I'm listening to their latest album, *Dixie Highway*, really loud, on headphones... *Endless Pride* (Yes! Absolutely!) and other songs. Otherworldly grandeur, a bit on the harder side, without denying their roots for a single second. Do we even need anything else?)

JESSICA - ALLMAN BROTHERS BAND
(Richard Betts)

Oh boy, a tough task... As one of the most influential and foundational bands, the Allman Brothers Band has churned out so many fantastic songs that the choice is darn difficult. They weren't exactly hitmakers in the traditional sense; instead, they specialized in live albums when that was still a rarity. They just wanted to play, play, play, and that's when they shone the brightest, in front of an ecstatic audience. Their tumultuous, tragic history never swayed them from their path. Co-founders of Southern Rock, or were they the founders? Although usually leaning towards the gentler, bluesier side, they always played with unwavering passion. Volumes could be written about them, and indeed, they have been.

With all due respect, praise, and admiration from nearly everyone, there might be a few naysayers who claim, "it all sounds the same, one album equals them all." Some other artists face that accusation, and once more, "nes" or "yo". You know what to expect – that's the "it all sounds the same" part, and you look forward to it. Many live albums are quite similar, they "overlap" – that's the second criticism. But for those who listen closely, they hear the subtle, fine, and sometimes significant differences and intricacies. Music is meant to be listened to.

The Allman Brothers Band recorded many, many of their countless concerts later on, immediately pressed them onto CDs, and sold them right after the show – an overwhelming number of CDs, each in very limited quantities. Their "official" albums are manageable, thankfully, still quite numerous, and some of those recorded gigs have made it into the "official" lineup. What's "official" and what's not – that's another topic.

Not hitmakers, yet their unmistakable sound and musical genius naturally produced some hits along the way. I could have chosen *Ramblin' Man*, their biggest hit by far, or others, but I've opted for **Jessica**, and it's not even a "song" because there are no vocals. But that's alright because, although quite pleasing and fitting, vocals usually play a somewhat subordinate role in the Allman Brothers Band, with their often more than 20-minute jams. **Jessica**, with its sparkling, flowing guitar work, is a catchy tune from the very first note, even without lyrics, and an excellent representation of the Allman Brothers Band's sound.

Which version should it be? The more than 7-minute album version, the approximately 4-minute single version, a more than 9-minute live version, or perhaps the 16-minute live version? Heck, I'd even go for 16 hours or more; you can bask in it for all eternity if you like.

KEY TO THE HIGHWAY – DEREK AND THE DOMINOS
(Segar, Broonzy)

The interlude of Derek and the Dominos is just another milestone in Eric Clapton's tumultuous and often tragic history. Derek and who? Clapton grew tired of always being in the spotlight as a superhero ("Clapton is God!") and just wanted to play in a band for a change.

But with Duane Allman by his side, he ended up with the next supergroup, and the other musicians certainly deserved the "super" label as well. There's plenty to read about how the name came about. Any lineup with Clapton is essentially a supergroup; that's his fate.

When I first listened to the double album *Layla And Other Assorted Love Songs*, I thought, "This isn't really my stuff." Maybe I still had too much Cream in my ears and Blind Faith in my head. It has since become one of my all-time favorite albums, and it's timeless!

Clapton and Allman on double lead guitar – it sends a delightful shiver down your spine, and I could have easily picked any song from this colossal album. It's a wonderfully swinging blues-rock masterpiece with subtle Southern undertones, and they've really emphasized the word "SONGS." Everyone knows *Layla*, maybe even more so in its later acoustic version. It was Clapton's heartache period, and he did end up marrying George Harrison's wife, Patti Boyd (though they later divorced), and becoming close friends with George... but that's another story.

I chose this almost ancient blues standard from 1940 (!) because Derek and the Dominos put their very "personal" stamp on it, and with this longest piece on the album, you have nearly 10 minutes to immerse yourself in this wonderful sound continuously.

Thankfully, many other songs on the album are not short either, often running 6 or 7 minutes long. By the way, the Steve Miller Band's version of **Key To The Highway** (see their own separate entry with another song) is also fantastic and completely different.

You have the key, and on this highway, you want to keep driving for all eternity!

LEADER OF THE PACK - SHANGRI-LAS

(George "Shadow" Morton, Jeff Barry, Ellie Greenwich)

An unforgettable teenage drama, "Heart-Ache-Love" of a different kind. With this song, the American girl group, consisting of two lovely pairs of sisters (one of them even twins), made their big international appearance and hit.

Betty loves the leader of a motorcycle gang, but her parents consider him a bad influence because he comes from the wrong side of town. They pressure her to break up with him, and in his disappointment, her lover speeds away and meets a fatal accident. It's a sad story with underlying social commentary, all in less than three minutes. One of the first songs to incorporate sounds other than just musical instruments and vocals – the roar of engines, screeching tires. Or was it the first of its kind? I won't delve deeper into that, but it's safe to say it was one of the earliest.

This fantastic blend of beat, engine noise, some spoken word, and a sound reminiscent of the late '50s/early '60s, as if Phil Spector had been involved (which he wasn't), along with the melodious, yearning voice of the lead singer, still gives me slight goosebumps and moist eyes, even more so than in earlier years... Is it a sign of mental aging?

In any case, the underlying social conflict remains as timeless as the quality of this short teenage drama.

LET'S WORK TOGETHER - CANNED HEAT
(Wilbert Harrison)

"Blues is the root of all rock music," you could say, and I say so too. This was also the belief of the two musicians, Alan Wilson and Bob Hite, who founded the band Canned Heat in Los Angeles in 1965, leading to considerable success at times. Even the name of the band is rooted in an old blues song.

Canned heat or simply sterno was, for some poor folks, a source of alcohol and a substitute for spirits that surely didn't do them any good. However, the songs of this band, always rooted in the blues, often with an airy feel, sometimes with a touch of country and a solid rock overlay, including forays into psychedelic territory – ideal for the hippie era – do a lot of good.

Almost everybody knows *On The Road Again* and *Goin' Up The Country*, but I've chosen **Let's Work Together** here, their biggest hit at least in the UK and possibly even better known worldwide. Originally released by the composer himself (a black blues musician – his *Kansas City*, among others, was also performed by the Beatles; at least sometimes something must be said about the composers) as *Let's Stick Together*, then released again by him in an edited version, Canned Heat set this wonderful song on fire in their own unique way.

A drum roll as a short introduction, wonderfully flowing guitar added, pumping bass, and then the slightly raspy voice of Bob the Bear (Bob "The Bear" Hite, who passed away much too soon), who has taken over the microphone here (instead of the usual Alan Wilson with his high but very pleasant "falsetto" voice), sets the tone – earthy, rocky, bluesy, all together.

"Together we stand, divided we fall ... let's work together..." that's the message, without the big pointing finger, which apparently fewer and fewer people seem to understand these days.

Despite an incredible number of lineup changes (with drummer Adolfo "Fito" de la Parra being the only almost-permanent original member, apart from the first album), the sterno is still burning, and some great guitarists got their calluses here (Harvey Mandel, Walter Trout). Although I unfortunately never saw/heard the almost-original lineup live, I consider myself lucky to have experienced the 2019 incarnation, with Fito, of course – the heat of the sterno still simmers mightily!

Often neglected in our times (unlike during the hippie era), *Let's Work Together* should be a motto for the future and certainly endures for eternity.

LEVITATION - HAWKWIND
(Brock)

Oh no, some might think – not Hawkwind, those space hippies who always sound alike! And everybody will think of *Silver Machine*, their only big and magnificent hit. Oh yes, I say – precisely Hawkwind, precisely because they always sound "alike," and because this glorious sound, this hypnotic space sound, allows you to ascend into higher realms that stretch into eternity. You don't need to be stoned or otherwise intoxicated (which is certainly not a hindrance but not my thing), just willing to listen and immerse yourself in the sound or let it lift you up.

Always alike, always the same – well, their sound is unmistakable, but those who listen closely will discover the differences and nuances, and some are only discovered after enjoying it countless times. Essentially more sound than song, it's difficult to pick out a specific one, but **Levitation** from the album of the same name certainly fits well thematically and is definitely one of their particularly outstanding pieces.

Furthermore, it's not entirely typical Hawkwind – unmistakably so, but the entire album leans noticeably towards the rock side, almost a unique feature in their impressive body of work (though there are still a few other "real barnstormers").

Despite the beloved bubbling, chirping, and spacey background noise, this one really rocks, driven by Ginger Baker's drums, who contributed his skills to this album. Lively, melodic, and fast-paced, with this excellent blend of sound and song, you can freely ascend – **Levitation** indeed!

By the way, the "splinter group" Hawklords, named after the Hawkwind album titled Hawklords, delights fans with ten excellent albums so far, sometimes a bit more rock-oriented and a bit less spacey, but with an unmistakable origin. And once again – a little secret tip for lovers of such sounds is Strobe, difficult to find or nearly impossible these days.

I just hope that Hawkwind continue forever – to this day, they still produce one excellent album after another, sometimes as the Hawkwind Light

Orchestra (which are, in a way, "solo projects" by Dave Brock, in the typical Hawkwind sound, of course). If you have one, you have them all – no, if you have them all (like me), as far as possible, you are one: well-prepared for eternity!

LOCOMOTIVE BREATH - JETHRO TULL
(Ian Anderson)

When I saw this (still) unknown band at the Marquee in London in 1967 or probably more like 1968 (I was there in both years, also in '69, and so on), with their medieval-dressed singer leaping and bounding across the stage like a mad dervish, swinging his flute and playing it standing on one leg like a flamingo, I knew: something big is coming our way!

A flute, that squeaky thing, as an instrument in a rock band? It surprisingly fit quite well, especially how Ian Anderson breathed new life into that metal rod, or rather blew life into it, in the literal sense. This absolutely unique, completely novel blend of pop, folk, jazz, rock, and blues elements was and still is a special hallmark and enrichment of the music scene like no other. Typical of the unmatched innovations of the 60s.

An unusual group with an unusual sound and an unusual name. Jethro Tull was a 17th and 18th-century English agricultural scientist – the choice of name suited the eccentric band leader with his love for country life.

Before I digress too far, I still want to share a few more words. The early albums were absolutely fantastic, even after the departure of Mick Abrahams (who went on to form the great band Blodwyn Pig), and then came *Aqualung*, Jethro Tull's best-selling album to this day. The religious (critical) and social themes and the previously unheard-of case (and still not again to this day? I can't think of anything), where both sides of the LP had their own titles, gave the impression of a concept album, which, according to the flutist's own words, it wasn't supposed to be.

I have sometimes "complained" here that choosing a song by a particular artist was especially difficult for me – this one definitely belongs to that category. *Locomotive Breath* was my first, direct choice ... but when I listened to the piece again after a long time, I had some doubts. I remembered it as more intense; *Aqualung* (the song) or *Living In the Past* came to mind.

In the end, I stuck with my initial choice – with the quiet, long piano intro that slowly picks up pace with some guitar accompaniment until that fierce, pounding riff takes over with the addition of drums and doesn't let up until the end, *Locomotive Breath* deserves this choice. Ian's distinctive voice is, of course, indispensable, and you wait in vain for a guitar solo, but the master once again shows what he can do with his flute.

Ian's expressive voice, which, with the subsequent albums and its always very similar phrasing, started to annoy me a bit. The once-great songs gradually merged into a homogenous blend in my ears, and I lost track of Jethro Tull for a long, long time, including Ian's solo albums. Solo or not, Jethro Tull is Ian Anderson, and vice versa. Oh, now some hardcore Jethro Tull fans will probably want to throttle me – this being said from someone who loves Rod Stewart or AC/DC, who always "sound the same"? Yes, he says so, musical tastes and listening preferences fortunately differ.

Just recently, I became aware that in 1987, some quite respectable music journalists chose the album *Crest Of A Knave* as the Heavy Metal Album of the Year, even ahead of Metallica. The internet is so handy... I listened briefly, and I bought it, my first Jethro Tull album since *Aqualung* (or *Living In The Past*, thereafter)! Heavy, yes, at least partly, Ian sounds somewhat different, and I'm happy to have "discovered" something again. Excellent, and I think I should also delve into some of the many, many later Jethro Tull albums. But "Heavy Metal Album of the Year" – that makes me wonder what those judges may have had in their tea...

In any case, Jethro Tull has rightfully left a big footprint in music history, and the locomotive may keep breathing and pounding for eternity.

LOOK AT YOURSELF - URIAH HEEP

(Hensley)

One of the very few bands with over 50 years under their belt, you have to place this group high up, despite many lineup changes, and although they were always somewhat in the "second league," they often had excellent quality to offer.

Their first album, ...*Very 'Eavy ...Very 'Umble*, wasn't all that heavy, and it wasn't all that humble either, and I must confess I shamefully neglected it back then. It already hinted at the direction from which many great hard rock songs would emerge. Heavy riffs, extended organ/instrumental passages, great guitar solos, melody, and dynamics. Sometimes ridiculed as the "poor man's Deep Purple," at least the basic comparison isn't entirely wrong when it comes to the pure music, although not the singers.

Uriah Heep never had rock shouters like Ian Gillan or David Coverdale, for example, but they always leaned on the "lighter" side, often associated with harmony vocals or slightly theatrical, which, not least, makes up their unique, sometimes even symphonic sound. Their subsequent works with the best songs of their entire career caught my attention, but not much more. It was only in recent years that I "rediscovered" Uriah Heep and realized what I had missed – a total of 24 great studio albums and 20 impressive live albums! It's something I can catch up on, and I'm working on it and making good progress. It was only a few years ago that I had the great pleasure of seeing them live for the first time, with the fantastic guitarist Mick Box as the only remaining original member and the outstanding singer Bernie Shaw, a fixture for over 30 years, who can definitely unleash his inner shouter from time to time. I hope the other great musicians will forgive me for not mentioning them by name here.

The departure of Ken Hensley (see there) after 10 years and 13 albums, who was responsible for many of their early great songs (especially as a composer, keyboardist, but also as a singer and guitarist), was a severe blow at the time, but it was compensated for, as were many other changes. Furthermore, Ken returned from time to time, and other illustrious musicians also passed through the band, underscoring their undeniable importance... as if they needed that.

To stick with the above-mentioned comparison – similar to Deep Purple, Uriah Heep are especially popular in Germany, they struggle in the USA and even in their own homeland, in contrast to Deep Purple. Could this be due to the "Wagnerian" power and sometimes melancholic, but always heavy music? Heavy, but not Heavy Metal, but rather top-notch Hard Rock (with fluid boundaries, as mentioned somewhere before), even to this day.

Absolutely top-notch, and once again, the agony of choice. Like most rocker colleagues, Uriah Heep are an album band, even though their folk-tinged *Lady In Black* was a big hit, especially in Germany, of course. It would definitely be a candidate for eternity, as would *Gypsy*, *Easy Livin'*, or the over 16-minute mega-opus *Salisbury* from the eponymous album, or *Magician's Birthday*, and so on... They also gave their distinctive style to some cover versions.

Just as much care as they put into their songs, Uriah Heep always paid great attention to their cover art, often featuring fantasy motifs (by Roger Dean, one of THE cover designers of the era, also for Yes and many others) and also horror themes. The mirrored aluminum foil on the album *Look At Yourself* was and still is a very special eye-catcher, and not least, the titular song *Look At Yourself* is exceptionally good, if you can say that in this context.

All the musical elements mentioned above come into play/hearing here, and even though Charles Dickens, the creator of the eponymous literary character, has long been dead, with this album, you can hold/listen to the mirror up to yourself for all eternity and get lost in it. If you don't want to see yourself, you should turn your listening gaze all the more towards Uriah Heep. First league. Eternal league.

MISSISSIPPI QUEEN - MOUNTAIN
(West, Laing, Pappalardi, Rea)

Tock, tock, tock sounds the cowbell... then that fat riff, followed by a fat lead guitar and fat vocals, it hits like a hammer, just like the entire first album by Mountain, which may argue with others about having significantly shaped or even invented the term Hard Rock. Not Heavy Metal, even though the boundaries are fluid (I repeat myself once again).

HARD ROCK, boldly written (and an inspiration for Deep Purple's phenomenal album *In Rock*), and perfectly suited for the "Fatty-Struwwelpeter" Leslie West, a rock, a mountain – his first solo album was called "Mountain," hardly noticed but noteworthy and certainly not without reference to his enormous body size.

He adopted this title as the name for his first group, which seemed to fill the gap left by Cream. However, it didn't quite fit, despite Leslie's admiration for Clapton and the fact that Felix Pappalardi, the producer of most Cream albums, played bass here and even lent his vocals. While Cream had Ginger Baker as one of the greatest drummers of all time, Leslie's lifelong buddy and companion, Corky Laing, was one of the... most unassuming, I'll say benevolently and with a friendly nod towards his parents. He didn't stand out too much, thanks to Leslie's guitar, did his job. Mountain – Leslie West – West, Bruce & Laing (Jack Bruce of Cream, among others), that's a massive sound mountain like no other, in which Leslie, with his raspy, gravelly voice and his "roast guitar," consistently follows and dominates the path set by the **Mississippi Queen**, providing great auditory pleasure. Sometimes more bluesy, occasionally a bit more delicate, but always "fat." Always similar, thankfully, but never truly "the same," as some ignorants might accuse him of being.

He's not fat these days, his straggly hair is gone, and he's lost half a leg. While this is unfortunate for him, it's not a great loss for the music scene, as long as he still has both hands and his raspy voice, and his output remains fat. Mostly as a solo artist or, occasionally, as Mountain again, with the fantastic (of course) album *Masters of War*, containing only songs by Bob Dylan (where Ozzy Osbourne also had a go at the mic) – but fat! And I've written about Bob Dylan in other places too.

A mountain takes (almost) forever to erode – may the Queen of the Mississippi reign until then, and beyond! [Very sadly so, only until December 23, 2020]

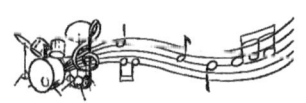

MOONLIGHT SHADOW –
MIKE OLDFIELD (FEAT. MAGGIE REILLY)
(Mike Oldfield)

Women are clearly underrepresented in this book; this is not intentional, but I am fully aware of it.

Similarly, I have deviated from the official notation here and added the name of the fantastic singer in this song, which is officially credited to Mike Oldfield (who also composed it) – credit where credit is due! Nothing said against Mike Oldfield, quite the opposite, and with great respect, especially for *Tubular Bells*, this gem has always been stored in my grey cells as "Maggie Reilly & Mike Oldfield."

Without Maggie's heavenly, crystal-clear voice, this wonderful song would be only half as wonderful – she carries it in perfect symbiosis with the acoustic (?) and electric guitar and synthesizer tones into emotionally resonant heights that make it hard to break away from. You just want to keep floating in this soft cushion that occasionally has a firmer substance.

From the beginning, on the mental set-list for this book, I was sure I had this song on some compilation, it's so familiar to me, and I love it so much. But no luck! So, I finally had to get the album – one of the few cases, or maybe the only one (?), where I bought a CD just for a single song. But it "compensates" (with bonus tracks, as is often the case these days) right away with three versions of this delightful earworm melody – the (unfortunately too short) single version, an "unplugged mix," and the longer (finally!) "12" maxi version.

The moon casts its shadow into eternity, and that is bliss times three. By the way, the rest of the CD is also quite good, with Roger Chapman and Ian Anderson as "featured singers."

MORE THAN A FEELING - BOSTON
(Tom Scholz)

Nomen est omen – music is more than a feeling and more than a song. If ever a band was associated with just one song, it's probably Boston with this very one (I've written something similar about at least one other band, please forgive me). This incomparable stroke of genius by Tom Scholz (the mastermind behind Boston, actually he is Boston) combines melody, sentimentality, and hard rock in a perfect, unique way. This mixture oozes, rocks, and drills its way into the ear canals and stays there, for all eternity, resistance is futile.

If that doesn't make your hair stand on end, I'd say you have 'no feeling'. It's almost cruel to unleash such a song on humanity. That voice, those guitars, that melody – compared to it, 'smooth as butter' is as hard as concrete, if you know what I mean.

You don't have to own all of Boston's few (only 6) albums (great logo!), mostly more or less derivatives of **More Than A Feeling** and more or less heavy (but I do, and have to). But everyone MUST have this song. Absolutely. Resistance is futile.

MR. TAMBOURINE MAN - THE BYRDS
(Bob Dylan)

The Byrds, these American birds with a "y" where you would expect an "i." In analogy to the Beatles with an "a" where you would expect an "e." Both names are new coinages that didn't exist until then.

When the Byrds stormed the international charts in the mid-60s with **Mr. Tambourine Man**, they were often compared to the Beatles, not least because of their distinctive mushroom haircuts, which were almost passé even among the music gods themselves at that time, having given way to longer locks. But musically, they had high-quality offerings to provide, setting trends for folk-rock with their delightful jingle-jangle sound (not dissimilar to that of the Searchers) and wonderful harmony singing, thus establishing the genre and giving the previously neglected 12-string guitar a new significance.

Despite subsequent hits and various good albums, the Byrds (all of whom were Beatles fans) couldn't live up to the high external expectations in the long run. Internal conflicts and many lineup changes were both the cause and the consequence. Nevertheless, they are definitely part of the aristocracy of music history, both as a band and as individual musicians among the many who passed through the band and left their significant marks as solo artists and/or in other formations.

This brings us back to the topic of composers. The Byrds were highly talented in this regard as well but also occasionally liked to reinterpret other compositions, which they gave a new spin to, and why not? Even the Beatles did that in their early years. One of their songs is honored elsewhere in this book (*Eight Miles High*), but **Mr. Tambourine Man** was once again an "external composition" that paved the way for a great, albeit brief, career.

I could repeat or point out what I have written about Bob Dylan in other places as a lyricist, artist, musician, namely... oh well, the reader can do that themselves!

May the tambourine man swing his instrument for all eternity, and as the Byrds let him do it in their heavenly and light-hearted way, he has nothing to fear in terms of competition.

MUSIC - JOHN MILES

(John Miles)

I can already hear the old rockers furrowing their brows again – John Miles, such a softie! But a softie who found the golden egg with this song.

Once again, it's an example of how an artist can immortalize themselves with just one song. Despite numerous albums and a few other minor hits, this equation is true: John Miles = **Music**; I don't want to do him any injustice.

Starting with gentle tones, including strings, he begins with a somewhat sweet but pleasant voice, stating right from the beginning: "Music was my first love, and it will be my last." But then things start to get going reasonably well, and he doesn't need to add many more words to his statement, why should he? Sometime in the mid-70s, somewhat off the current trend of the time, success justified him.

Mostly an instrumental track with quite a few tempo changes, going back and forth between slow string passages and beautiful, lively guitar sounds, **Music** is an ode to the love of music that gets under your skin if you allow it. Just the sentence quoted above is etched in stone for eternity, and not even a syrupy undertone, even if somewhat thickened with a few lumps, can shake that stone.

As a perennial participant in the "Night of the Proms" (not my thing), John Miles continues to thrive on this enlightenment to this day, and he's more than entitled to it... and perhaps it's an opportunity for me to delve (back) into his work a bit more.

If anyone accuses me of having a certain penchant for schmaltz, sentimentality, and kitsch, they're not entirely wrong, but I can live with that. "Music was my first love" – and it will remain loyal to me until the end of my life and into eternity.

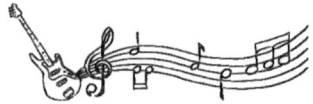

NEEDLES AND PINS - THE SEARCHERS
(Jack Nitzsche, Sonny Bono)

In the "Mersey Beat" aftermath of the Beatles, this wasn't the first No. 1 hit in the UK for the Searchers (that was *Sweets for My Sweet*). But their almost sweet-sounding harmony vocals and their breezy, swinging guitar sound shine particularly well here, I believe. The Searchers looked "good," also hailed from Liverpool, and rightfully enjoyed chart success for a while. The Searchers (not to be confused with the Seekers, who also left behind some very nice "Folk-Beat" numbers – similar names with a similar but slightly different meaning) didn't have the songwriting talent of the Beatles, but they had the talent to elevate the songs of other composers with their wonderful singing and heavenly guitar playing.

I chose this song here, but it could have easily been *Sugar And Spice*, *What Have They Done To The Rain*, *When You Walk In The Room*, or the aforementioned song, among others. A firm place in the eternal annals of music history is assured.

Even some later songs with a changed lineup still capture that "Searchers feeling" quite closely, which is quite remarkable.

NIGHTS IN WHITE SATIN – THE MOODY BLUES

(Justin Hayward)

Their number one hit *Go Now*, at the height of the Beat boom, once again seemed to confirm the motto "nomen est omen." There were a few smaller hits that followed, but generally speaking, the Moody Blues disappeared from the scene for several years.

That changed abruptly with their second album *Days Of Future Past*, which also immediately changed their style from R&B-influenced pop-rock of a rather superior kind to symphonically influenced prog-rock of a very special kind.

A milestone for progressive rock and concept albums, the album they composed themselves describes the events of a day, with a spoken intro (and outro) presented in a "classical" instrumental intro. The overall sound is very orchestral – the complete credit reads "The Moody Blues with the London Festival Orchestra," although the second part is written in smaller letters.

The Beat and Rock fans must have felt like they were in the wrong movie or as if they had put on the wrong record. But the concept worked, very successfully, and provided a counterpoint in those hippie and flower power times, fitting in strangely with its often delicate tones as well.

Especially the closing song, **Nights In White Satin**, is slightly sentimental, beautifully melodic, a first-rate love ballad that deservedly achieved hit status in a shortened single version, or several of them. Perhaps not as big as *Go Now*, but over the decades (!), it has repeatedly (due to being "re-released" several times) and overall probably had a greater impact than their first hit.

And yes, this album also appealed to the less narrow-minded Beat and Rock fans and laid the foundation for a successful career for the band, whose members also pursued somewhat less successful but very intriguing solo careers, in which the distinctive melody and skillful simplicity sometimes took a backseat.

The days of the future have passed, and the nights sway in white satin, this is how eternity could look.

NINE MILLION BICYCLES - KATIE MELUA
(Mike Batt)

A strange title for a love song, but if you listen, the nine million bicycles find their place. And with this song, I'm diving deep into the realm of cuddly music. The composer, Mike Batt, is a versatile talent, having written many hits for various artists, working as an arranger, producer, conductor of symphonic orchestras... and he's also the "discoverer" of Katie Melua.

With relatively few hits, the pretty British singer of Georgian descent has sung her way into the hearts of listeners worldwide (and earned herself a hefty bank account, which is well-deserved), and especially this song softens every heart and gives me a big goosebump.

With a slight Asian touch in the melody (the nine million bicycles are in Beijing), this dreamy sound world flows gently, and if someone isn't enchanted by it, there's no helping them.

If there were angels, and they had voices, they would sound like Katie Melua, I'm convinced of that – and the fact that an asteroid was named after her fits perfectly! It drifts through the universe forever, just as this musical dream captivates you eternally, not only until nine million bicycles have zoomed by, even though that might take a while...

NO MORE WALKS IN THE WOOD /
/ HOW LONG - EAGLES

(Don Henley, Stewart Smith & John Hollander // J. D. Souther)

Oh, a little cheat here, these are "actually" two songs. Let me explain a bit more.

Eagles, everyone immediately thinks of *Hotel California*, their eternal and eternally wonderful mega-hit. But in this case, I haven't chosen the obvious, I can do things differently too.

After interruptions and, as one heard, rather nasty disputes over rights and large sums of money, the Eagles rose to new heights in 2007 with the phenomenal double album *Long Road Out Of Eden*. Or, to put it differently, the less harmony there was in the earlier band dynamics, the better the harmony in their later singing and playing.

Exceptions prove the rule – so in this case, and with this exceptional album, I'm bending the rules a bit. The first track seamlessly transitions into the second, so I can allow myself this trick. It feels like an overture followed by the main performance. Also, the total duration of just (unfortunately) five and a half minutes justifies considering it as "one" song.

No More Walks In The Wood is a heavenly, hauntingly beautiful a cappella piece, despite the very sparse, occasional acoustic guitar in the background. In this song, the Eagles, reduced to a quartet, once again demonstrate their harmony skills. And as soon as the last note fades, the guitars and other instruments kick in with **How Long** in classic Southern style, delivering a performance that will make your speakers shake, and the harmony singing remains at the same high level. This applies to the entire album.

Two goosebump-inducing moments at the beginning of the album, which slowly wane a bit but continually tingle anew. A mature, refined, perfect, and unexpectedly high-quality late work from this fantastic group with the motto "Quality over quantity." Hopefully, it won't be their last.

No more walks in the wood, and **How long**... these questions may be answered by eternity. Until then, you can immerse your ears in this "one" or "two" song/s and more.

NOTHING ELSE MATTERS - METALLICA
(Hetfield, Ulrich)

The comparison is certainly a bit unconventional and far-fetched, but Metallica could also be somewhat described as the "Beatles" of heavy metal. They were the ultimately foundational band for this music genre (Black Sabbath, Deep Purple, Led Zeppelin, etc., were more on the hard rock side, though the boundaries are fluid) that shook up the world in the early 80s.

Their initial successes in Germany owed a not insignificant portion to my former company, Wishbone Records*, before they became too big but still formed a solid basis for my business. Metallica managed to evolve with only minor lineup changes, going beyond enthusiastic headbanging to write songs that stuck in the shaken ear.

This is especially true for their *Black Album* (in analogy to the Beatles' *White Album*, which many consider their masterpiece – wrong, each of their albums is a masterpiece), a milestone not only for heavy metal. If someone doesn't like this music genre, they should perhaps listen to this album; it might change their opinion.

Heavy, weighty, as black as a meteorite striking the Earth. Not mindless headbanging, as enjoyable as it may be. Heavy melodies. Heavy music, lead-heavy and a poison like lead when it gets into your blood – a wonderful poison.

Other hard rockers and metalheads have created many beautiful love ballads, but none as lead-heavy, yet invigorating, and sometimes even gentle as Metallica with **Nothing Else Matters**.

Eternity may be black, but anything else doesn't matter...

* https://de.wikipedia.org/wiki/Wishbone_Records

OH WELL (PARTS 1 & 2) - FLEETWOOD MAC

(Peter Green)

Well, which Fleetwood Mac song should it be? There are several milestones to choose from, and I won't even start listing them now.

For me, this phenomenal group exists in two forms. With all due respect, I only consider the first, the original incarnation with only a few subtle lineup changes, as "phenomenal." This lineup had some great hits, but the truly "phenomenal" commercial success came after the metamorphosis into Fleetwood Mac II, at which point I, with repeated respect, turned my back on the group. These lineup changes were not gradual but rather marked a significant change in direction.

Hits were not the primary goal, I argue, of Peter Green's Fleetwood Mac, as they were initially known; they happened almost incidentally. Earthy, wild British blues was their flag, and Fleetwood Mac set standards, especially Peter Green with his unmatched guitar playing, often using the slide guitar. For those who don't know what that means... well, just listen.

In **Oh Well**, the Dobro was also used. For those who don't know... see above. Starting rather quietly and almost acoustically, a fat riff soon kicks in. The vocals are more like spoken words, unusual for the time, and the short lyrics hint at or foreshadow Peter Green's penchant for religious sects, into which he unfortunately sank, aided by drugs, yet he still released one or two good solo albums.

More of an instrumental piece than a "song," it then becomes much quieter, almost fading away. But flip the single over, and it continues wonderfully melodic, purely instrumental and calm for about five more minutes, somewhat in the style of their great hits like *Man of the World* or *Albatross*. Well, I did end up mentioning a few.

On a longplayer, **Oh Well** was released somewhat later as part of the fantastic (of course) album *Then Play On*. At that time, the different US/UK versions of albums were already becoming less common, but not quite. **Oh Well** was consistently audible on later compilations without the need to "flip it over."

Oh Well is a good essence of both sides of the first Fleetwood Mac coin back then, with neither being as pop-oriented as Fleetwood Mac II.

Alright, Peter Green managed to overcome his setbacks and lulls somehow, still occasionally tours, and has earned a place for eternity, exemplified by this earworm. [He's now *In The Skies*, as his second solo album was called. Unfortunately, he passed away after writing this entry, now touring in eternity.]

Oh Well has also been frequently covered and provides good material for both roaring metal/hard rock versions and soft-played acoustic variations, or even a mix of both.

Oh Well...

ONLY YOU (AND YOU ALONE) - PLATTERS
(Buck Ram)

A leap back to the 1950s, the heyday of vocal groups, especially in the USA.

The singing is what makes the music, with the background instruments played by professional studio musicians, who were probably often paid only a small fee. (It wasn't until the 1990s with "boy groups" like Take That, etc., and "girl groups" like the Spice Girls that this tradition was revived, and whether the instrumental musicians were better compensated then, I don't know, but I suspect not.)

Created some years before my "Big Bang" (the Beatles), this song only found its way onto my turntable several years later – anyone who engages with music can't avoid it.

A deep dive into the treasure trove of sentimental songs, remarkable in many ways, this "tearjerker" softens even the hardest of hearts.

A simple love song, perhaps the best of all time, in which the then lead singer, Tony Williams of this "classic" lineup, infuses his "O-o-only Youhuhhu" with such soulful and heart-rending emotion that… as mentioned before, hearts are softened.

It was highly remarkable that a "group of niggers" (I'll put it as bluntly as many Americans felt in that racially charged era, and unfortunately still do today) topped the charts, shockingly so, especially with a woman in their ranks!

It was also the heyday of rock 'n' roll, and the wonderful harmonies of the Platters found their way into and served as templates for many a rock 'n' roll hit. It was deservedly not their only big success, and perhaps they paved the way for other black musicians to some extent. If there's one stereotype, it's this: Black people have an unmatched sense of music; not everyone of them, but many, and many more than people of other "races". It doesn't make them better than others (all people are equal... good or bad), but it's a reason to be especially proud.

I'm getting off track here; this is about music. With his cover version many years later, Ringo didn't even try to cover that fervor but turned it into a casual sing-along, swing-along piece – I'll say "without judgment."

With countless lineup changes and legal disputes, the Platters still exist in one form or another, or rather in several, and I'm sure they all manage the legacy well, which, of course, includes other magnificent songs. **Only You (And You Alone)** – only this song will melt stones for eternity.

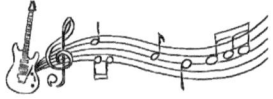

PHOENIX - WISHBONE ASH
(Turner, Upton, Turner, Powell)

Lead guitar, rhythm guitar, bass, drums, and vocals, that was and still is the common formula for a "band." Not so with Wishbone Ash. Two guitars, why not two lead guitars as well? The concept was not entirely new (Beck/Page with the Yardbirds, Allman Brothers Band), but no group has embraced it as intensely and succinctly as Wishbone Ash, which is why they are not entirely unjustified in being considered the "inventors" of the twin-guitar sound (different to double-guitar).

The leads don't just take turns; they often play together, intertwining and complementing each other. The concept of chorus, chorus, solo, etc., is also set aside by Wishbone Ash. Their songs are often almost a double-guitar solo, better twin-gutiar solo, from beginning to end, which evident right from their overwhelming debut album in 1970, providing a new listening and musical experience.

To this day, the typical and unmistakable Wishbone Ash sound persists despite many lineup changes, and only Andy Powell remains as the original member performing on stages around the world, with occasional new and always good albums.

Wishbone Ash is one of my absolute favorite bands, at least in the top ten, and I've seen/heard no other band live more times; two hands are far from enough. But I'll stop before I get too carried away.

Many songs by Wishbone Ash are truly timeless, and I won't even start listing them; instead, I must and want to make my choice. Singing was never their strength, although Andy improved and became more confident over the years. But who needs vocals when we have these two guitars with their pleasantly sharp, high notes over a solid, competent bass-drum foundation that blows through the brain?

Starting with a drum roll and gently introducing guitars, fat bass, **Phoenix** steadily builds, and the sparse singing is used more like an instrument, barely justifying the term "song" – one could also say that the singing doesn't disturb the guitar storm of this "instrumental" piece. Breaks, tempo changes – once again, a lesson in dynamics. And guitars, guitars... this original version can be enjoyed for a little over 10 minutes, and since then, in many live versions with different guitarists at Andy's side (and released on live albums), sometimes lasting 20 minutes or more, always fantastic, always different, and a staple of their live performances for 50 years.

So, choosing this song by Wishbone Ash cannot be entirely wrong; the **Phoenix** will rise from the ashes again and again for eternity!

RED HOT - ROBERT GORDON

(William Emerson)

The 70s are gradually entering the final stretch, Glam Rock is in vogue, Punk is casting its shadow ahead, and then Robert Gordon appears – pompadour hairstyle, Western shirt... wasn't that popular about 20 years ago?

The addition of "... with Link Wray" already hints that we're not 20 years too late, and for Rock 'n' Roll, it's never too late anyway. On his first album, Robert Gordon presents Rock 'n' Roll standards in a modern way, thanks in no small part to Link Wray, with a voice straight out of the best of the 50s, including the timeless *Summertime Blues*.

But most importantly, the very first track, **Red Hot**, kicks off so energetically that no eye can stay dry and no leg can remain still. It's a Rock 'n' Roll masterclass, an essence of this fundamental style, with fantastic drum fills, guitar riffs, and honky-tonk piano. Anyone who can sit still while listening to it must be deaf or paralyzed.

I haven't followed Robert Gordon further, I must admit to my shame. It's something I should add to my to-do list. Just as short and snappy as this gem of a track is this entry.

But with this, you can rock out timelessly and endlessly until the floor glows **Red Hot**.

RIDERS ON THE STORM - THE DOORS
(The Doors)

Ha, with this band, everyone would have surely expected *Light My Fire*, but I can also surprise. Okay, *Light My Fire* wouldn't be a bad choice, neither would *The End* (an excellent soundtrack to the equally excellent film Apocalypse Now, and not to be confused with the Beatles song of the same name) or some other fantastic songs by The Doors, like *L.A. Woman*, and so on...

Unfortunately, The Doors were granted only a relatively short window of time, abruptly cut short by the tragic death of Jim Morrison. Attempts by the three surviving band members to keep The Doors open were met with less success. The albums with Jim Morrison constitute an impressive body of work, and their creative output is an indispensable legacy.

These **Riders on the Storm** create a very special atmosphere with their gently swaying background and Jim Morrison's ever-charismatic vocals, complete with thunder and lightning.

Strangely, this song isn't stormy at all, and the riders move rather leisurely ahead. Perhaps it's this contrast that creates the magic. In calmness lies the strength for eternity.

If someone doesn't feel captivated by this, they should ignite their own fire; perhaps that will help them kick open some doors.

SABRE DANCE - LOVE SCULPTURE

(Aram Khachaturian, arr. Edmunds)

Wales is England's rural backyard, but it proved that it has outstanding musicians too, not least the Love Sculpture trio in the late 1960s with its only two gigantic albums, criminally neglected and ahead of its time.

The head of the group and an "axe swinger" par excellence was Dave Edmunds, who could almost make every speaker burst with his guitar thunder. A prime example of such a storm is this **Sabre Dance**, once again not a "song" but an overflowing instrumental piece based on a "classical" composition. (By the way, "classical" in my sense generally refers to the music discussed in this book. Period.)

For eleven and a half minutes, Dave lets his guitar dance in a way that had hardly been heard before, not only on this virtuoso ride. Comparisons with Hendrix, Clapton, Beck, Page, and so on place him on a level with these heroes. Driven by bass and drums, he swirls with the sabres, uh, I mean with his "axe," leaving you both in awe of what you're hearing and seeing. No, hearing shouldn't go away; on the contrary, your ears will just wiggle with excitement! In a shortened form, the sabres even danced high up in the British charts.

Despite receiving good reviews but only having moderate commercial success, Dave Edmunds, the jack-of-all-trades, didn't let it deter him. He turned to rockier pop music as an artist, songwriter, producer, and multi-instrumentalist. He had hits like *I Hear You Knocking* and others, released great albums, and played a significant role in the emerging Pub Rock scene. Another highly deserved success story.

And these sabre guitars, or guitar sabres, are dancing irresistibly into eternity.

SAN FRANCISCO - SCOTT MCKENZIE
(John Phillips)

Many songs bear the name of the alleged or actual hippie capital, San Francisco, in their title, but none as short and concise as this one (with its lengthy subtitle in parentheses: "Be Sure to Wear [Some] Flowers in Your Hair").

Just as short as the main title was the singer's career, but he secured a place for himself in eternity with it, can proudly claim one of the best-selling singles of the 1960s, and has gone down in the annals of music history.

THE summer song of 1967, this wonderful melody with its airy and light swinging guitar sound, accompanied by a relaxed beat and some chimes, and layered with Scott's very pleasant, soothing voice, inevitably embeds itself in the auditory nerves and brain folds. One wants to float away and forever linger in/on this island of happiness called **San Francisco**. It stimulates the auditory nerves and all others to a tingling activity – we may not be able to fly like geese, except in our thoughts, but we can emulate their carefree spirit...

This song smells, tastes, and above all, sounds like freedom and boundless well-being; it breathes them, as perhaps only possible during the Flower Power era.

Though not written by Scott McKenzie himself, but by John Phillips of the Mamas and the Papas (see there), who also plays here, this divine song must have been sufficient to make Scott McKenzie's (✝ 2012) life enjoyable, which is/was sincerely granted to him.

SEE EMILY PLAY - PINK FLOYD
(Syd Barrett)

I believe that with no other artist did I find the choice of a song as challenging as with Pink Floyd (haha, I've written this before), one of the greatest "mega-acts" of all time. Despite the combined names of two blues musicians, these London guys had very little to do with blues – their unusual creations were far ahead of their time from the very beginning. Entrenched in the world's memory (which is a level above world music memory) just like The Beatles, who remain unsurpassed at the top, with The Rolling Stones and a few others following closely, there's little need to say much about Pink Floyd here.

Nevertheless, I still want to chat a bit more. The first two hits, *Arnold Layne* and *See Emily Play*, not only caught my attention but also introduced new sounds in the immensely rich and innovative 60s. I listened to their first album, *The Piper at the Gates of Dawn*, at least partially in a "listening booth" (similar to a phone booth) at the legendary HMV Shop on Oxford Street... and was somewhat disappointed. In these booths, you could even play the records yourself, wonderful times! Maybe I had skipped the two brilliant tracks, *Astronomy Domine* and *Interstellar Overdrive*, or wasn't quite ready for them, I don't know, and the other unusual tracks as well. Both of the mentioned tracks later appeared even more magnificently on *Ummagumma*.

However, with that double album, I became an absolute PF disciple, embracing all their works. I saw them perform live many times in the early years and later with their overwhelming multimedia stage shows. One of their concerts on the Côte d'Azur was, in a way, also multimedia, with speakers distributed in the trees all around – true surround sound! And I was lucky to be there.

Pink Floyd were never really focused on hits; they found their hits in the increasingly important album charts, which they dominated. With *The Dark Side of the Moon* and *Wish You Were Here*, they broke many records that still stand today. These albums and others provide plenty of material for eternity.

In the end, I chose **See Emily Play** because, despite its brevity compared to later compositions, this song already encapsulates everything that defines the group ("Pink Floyd in a nutshell," as you would say). Rock, rhythm, spacey sounds, wonderful often light melodies with a touch of melancholy, dynamism – the typical, absolutely unique Pink Floyd mixture in its purest form.

What's particularly noteworthy is that this song was composed by founding member Syd Barrett, who paved the way that was never abandoned, even though he left the band shortly thereafter, became a psychiatric case, and had little commercial success with his later solo albums but became a living legend (which, in a way, ended with his death in 2006 but still persists). Before he left, David Gilmour had already joined, briefly making the group a quintet.

Apart from The Beatles, there are probably no other groups with more cover bands that, as you hear and read, sometimes perfectly reproduce the original. My memories of the originals suffice for me. And similar to The Beatles or The Who, despite their completely different music, the same applies to Pink Floyd: Only these four members (after Syd Barrett), no others, even though Roger Waters later left the group, make up the band. Additional studio or live musicians were always hired, never members.

It's an endless pleasure to see – and hear – Emily playing with these magnificent sounds for all eternity!

SEPTEMBER PARTS 1 & 2 – PETER & THE TEST TUBE BABIES
(Peter & The Test Tube Babies)

I'm not a big punk fan, although I do appreciate punk music and its influences (even if some might raise an eyebrow at the mention of "punk music").

When it comes to punk songs, it's a bit of a different story – it's punk, after all...

But in punk, (almost) anything goes, so I'm not ashamed to bend the rules a bit here, merging two songs, or song parts, into one. On the album with the brilliant cover and an equally brilliant title, *The Mating Sounds Of South American Frogs*, there are **September Part 1** and **September Part 2**, technically two songs.

At first, you might think the record is broken because there's no sound, until slowly, very slowly, you start to hear the croaking mating sounds of South American (I assume) frogs, accompanied by the chirping of crickets. It gets louder and louder, drums kick in, buzzing, whirring guitar riffs take over, and a bold, contrasting riff blasts over it all, drowning out the frogs' croaks. It's a feast for any guitar fan. Peter lets us know that he can't wait any longer (for what, we're not quite sure), and if you want to revel in this sound even more, you're in for a bitter disappointment after a minute and a half.

But wait! That was Part 1, an appetizer. After 10 more strong tracks – with a hefty mix of punk and a good dose of rock that really hits the ears – Part 2 comes as the final track. It continues with the pumping bass, the wonderfully buzzing guitar play, and the brutal contrasting riffs. Peter reminds us once or twice more that he can't wait, and fortunately, the journey continues with these marvelous sounds. The tempo gradually slows down, transitioning into something completely uncharacteristic of punk, almost psychedelic, and then the frogs make their presence known again.

After a moment of silence, a loud "croak" (which sounds like a big fart) serves as the final punctuation mark.

I certainly won't wait until September to listen to this masterpiece again. I could listen to this guitar feast forever, with or without frogs.

As for whether the frogs received their royalties, I don't know – perhaps they got an extra serving of flies.

SOMETIMES I FEEL LIKE SCREAMING - DEEP PURPLE

(Ian Gillan, Roger Glover, Jon Lord, Steve Morse, Ian Paice)

In some cases, it's inevitable that an artist or group appears twice here. This monster track is one of those cases – from the album *Purpendicular*, 26 years after *Deep Purple in Rock* with *Child in Time* (see there). And for me, these are also the two best Deep Purple albums, although all of them are great, with some nuances, and absolutely essential. They seem to never stop bringing deep purple happiness. [Just recently, their latest work *Turning to Crime* was released – another fantastic album!]

Almost in the same lineup as *Child in Time*, except that now (until recently) Steve Morse had taken over the role of Ritchie Blackmore. Hardcore Ritchie Blackmore fans may want to throw stones at me, and I hold him in high regard, but I consider Steve to be the best guitarist Deep Purple has ever had – and one of the best in his field anyway, period.

Similar to *Child in Time*, the piece starts off gently. You can hear the years in Ian Gillan's voice, but in a positive sense. Then it kicks off, occasionally calming down a bit, then getting wild again – and almost from the beginning, Steve's guitar licks dig deep into your bones, including the consuming solo, repeating almost to the point of no return, and it's incredibly powerful! Ian can still scream almost as wonderfully as before.

I can't find better words to describe it than quoting myself (translated here) from my autobiography*:

"Steve Morse's repetitive guitar solo still tears me apart, every time I hear this brilliant masterpiece, it dissects my skin into every single cell, cuts my heart, soul, and brain into pieces, makes tears flow, my back and shoulders tense up – unique! Tears aren't always a sign of sadness and unhappiness, but also of joy, happiness, and enthusiasm, especially with such unique works of art.

In other words, and to put it more concisely: it blows my mind away! Sounds crazy, but it's true. Somehow, these tones seem to randomly invade

my psyche like a single key to Fort Knox's high-security vault; my synapses celebrate Christmas, Easter, birthdays, and the first time having sex together. Achieving this overwhelming reaction is only accomplished by a very few other pieces, at least to some extent. You have to listen to it LOUD. Maybe that will wake me up from the not-so-distant grave (hopefully still a long way off)."
Another opus (of the few) that should be played at my funeral.

* Ferdinand Köther: Ich glaube an Hühner / BoD, ISBN 978-3-739206356

SPACE ODDITY - DAVID BOWIE
(David Bowie)
Bowie, the chameleon... and of course, his real name wasn't actually Bowie, but that's true for many other artists as well (that they adopted a stage name).
His very first hit catapulted him into eternity, into the infinity of the cosmos. Inspired by the mega-film *2001: A Space Odyssey*, Bowie slightly modified the title and wrote and sang an opus for eternity, with a barely audible acoustic intro and slight Pink Floyd-like elements, without really "borrowing."
On the contrary, David Robert Jones, alias Bowie, set some trends or at least influenced them, and

you could never predict what to expect from him, hence his nickname. This unpredictability was his trademark, and perhaps a reason why, despite having high respect, I was never a big fan, although I appreciate many of his other great songs that he composed and performed.

Maybe he himself never really knew where he stood or where the journey should go, and in the process, he left behind some milestones but also some less noteworthy works.

A big star in the pop-rock sky, whose oddity, with this haunting song about the lonely journey into nowhere for all eternity in the universe, is firmly anchored and hints at the ruthless infinity...

STAIRWAY TO HEAVEN - LED ZEPPELIN
(Page, Plant)

Oh, Led Zeppelin, once again a significant reason for me to lament. Not about Led Zeppelin, quite the opposite, but about choosing a song from this absolutely unparalleled, genre-defining band.

But what am I telling you? Everyone knows this, although it might have receded into the background nowadays. Almost every one of their songs, or many of them, has the quality of an "eternity song" – maybe not necessarily from their later albums, which unquestionably also have their great class, that's Led Zeppelin for you.

I've identified with hardly any other band more (except for the Beatles, of course, but they weren't just a "band" – they were the Beatles), and apart from Wishbone Ash, I probably haven't seen any other band live as often. The first time was in 1969 at the Marquee in London (like many other concerts described in my German book*), and the last time was at the Westfalenhalle in Dortmund in 1980 (it was terrible), relatively shortly before Bonzo's death, and thus the death of the band. And in between, of course, several times.

Their first album already made a huge impact, was a bombshell, followed by others, and who, apart from Pink Floyd, could afford to release an album without a name on the cover!? (Even on the Beatles' *White Album*, the name was presented in majestic lettering.)

This album was the fourth and is often referred to as *Led Zeppelin IV* (the first was simply *Led Zeppelin*). It contains this fantastic, epic song, perhaps THE Led Zeppelin song, and maybe some are now disappointed with my choice because it's so obvious.

But "obvious," "widely known," etc., doesn't mean "bad" or "less good." The contemplative, acoustic intro with an unusual flute (or synth?) for Led Zeppelin, Robert's, as always, penetrating, intense vocals, the progression, step by step, staircase by staircase, that he ascends to the heavens with his angelic blond locks, and Jimmy's resounding guitar solo at the end – all of this gives you goosebumps for 8 minutes. Although never released as a single, **Stairway to Heaven** is probably Led Zeppelin's biggest hit, the album certainly was, like all the others. [Very recently, just before printing: The allegation of plagiarism, supposedly "stolen" from the song *Taurus* by the group Spirit, has been definitively dismissed. Good.]

The fantasy lyrics can be interpreted one way or another (or not at all), but anyone who climbs this staircase to heaven wishes it could go on into eternity, higher and higher, the sky is infinitely far away...

---

* Ferdinand Köther: Ich glaube an Hühner / BoD,
ISBN 978-3-739206356

STARLESS - KING CRIMSON

(Cross, Fripp, Wetton, Palmer-James)

As mentioned elsewhere or for the first time here, if you haven't read the other part, I can't avoid featuring some artists (two, to be precise) twice.

Just like *Epitaph* (see there), **Starless** by King Crimson is not a "hit" in terms of charts, but a monumental opus (more than 12 minutes long) that should be in every music collection, I say.

It starts so beautifully, melodic and gentle, soon joined by John Wetton's wonderfully powerful voice. It slowly builds, then recedes with sparkling bass and guitar runs (I don't want to invoke dynamics again...), mellotron, accentuated percussion elements. It keeps building, building (no one's singing anymore), screeching noises join the fray, and it keeps building. A saxophone, pleasantly and jazzy shrill, adds to the commotion. A break, even more screeching noises above all other instruments, chaos breaks out, and it takes strong nerves to continue listening.

Then this wonderfully transparent melody that resolves the chaos, rich and bold, just before you'd like to turn off the power to escape this auditory storm – music is hard to describe with words. A marvelous, indescribable (did I mention that already) contrast, and by the end, your ears and nerves feel somewhat like the cat that was released from the washing machine.

Essentially an instrumental piece, this track is a quintessential King Crimson work, the essence. Despite frequent lineup changes (always the best of the best), it delivers the unmistakable King Crimson sound in its highest form, thanks to the mastermind Robert Fripp.

Starless is not for the faint-hearted and for ears only accustomed to pop. "Starless and Bible Black..." (excerpt from the sparse lyrics) – the soundtrack for eternity, one you can indulge in or run away from screaming, even though there have been no stars anymore in the sky for a long time.

STILL I'M SAD - YARDBIRDS

(Paul Samwell-Smith, Jim McCarty)

Which band can claim to have had three of the greatest guitarists of all time in their ranks? This honor belongs to the Yardbirds or "chickens" – it was a bit of a chicken coop in terms of their high-caliber personnel. In and out, pecking included.

In the context of their not so numerous (but wonderful) hits during the heyday of the Beat Boom, **Still I'm Sad** is absolutely atypical, both for the time and the group itself, and it reaches far ahead to the Gregorian chant that briefly became "trendy" in the pop world a few decades later.

This entrancing, echoing choir singing defines the piece, an exotic element in the colourful, poppy charts of the time. Without remarkable accents from Jeff Beck (their lead guitarist at that time), the enchanting, sorrowful-melancholic melody sneaks into your ears and brain as a complete work of art.

A hauntingly beautiful Yardbirds song for eternity, and before I start writing even more about the Yardbirds, I'd better stop, because otherwise, the clucking won't end... but I'm not sad, I'm happy that they created this beautiful song.

STRANGLEHOLD - TED NUGENT

(Ted Nugent, Rob Grange)

Ted Nugent is an arsehole. I'll just say it like that, he won't read it, but if he does, all the better.

I'm not talking about his Tarzan antics; that can be quite entertaining – it rocks, and Tarzan is okay. But I can't describe someone who's an NRA supporter, a gun enthusiast, and a big game hunter in any other way.

Has anyone ever noticed that all these so-called "hunters" these days aren't really hunters but rather cowardly animal killers with a pure lust for murder? They only shoot their defenseless prey from a safe distance. "Conservation and care" – nonsense. Nature conserves and cares for itself, and humanity disrupts it more than enough... different topic, I'm digressing.

Here, it's about music, and if you only consider that, Ted Nugent is a very noteworthy rocker. Period. Many strong songs and albums, but the first song on his first solo album, following a remarkable career start with the Amboy Dukes, is unparalleled.

The guitar intro rocks, and then, accompanied by powerful drums, that wonderfully rolling, rocking (Rock 'n' Roll, after all) guitar lick starts, repeating itself, a fantastic solo, and the dynamic and melody I love are not lacking either. Ted Nugent contributes a bit to the vocals but mostly leaves it to someone who can do it better, focusing on his musical weapon.

Despite the martial title **Stranglehold** (aha, Ted Nugent...), and the equally martial lyrics (but even Paul McCartney wrote a song called **Stranglehold**), this is a rocker par excellence that can put you in an auditory ecstasy for more than 8 minutes, or in other words, it takes your ears in a stranglehold. In this case, I'm more than happy to be a defenseless victim forever and ever.

Ted Nugent should stick to shooting and hitting bullseyes with his guitar; he can do that wonderfully without shooting himself in the foot or any harmless prey.

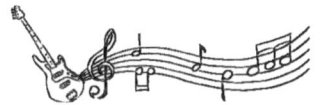

SUMMERTIME - BRAINBOX

(George Gershwin, DuBose Heyward, Ira Gershwin)

Not only does travel broaden the mind, but writing books (and reading them) does too.

I used to think that *Yesterday* by the Beatles was the most covered song of all time, with around 3,000 versions, and many people think that (and a friend of mine has that many). Far from it – this musical song (from Porgy & Bess) dates back to the '50s... no, wait, let me correct that! It's from the '30s, unbelievably, Billie Holiday had a hit with it as early as 1936!

There are allegedly about 25,000 to 30,000 versions of **Summertime**, and that's been the case since the 1930s up to the 2020s, and I'm sure it will continue well beyond. If this isn't a qualification for a song to be considered for "eternity," then I don't know what would be required for such a qualification. This record (even though I have my slight doubts – it also depends on the interpretation of a "version") will probably remain unmatched for eternity.

Often, or even most of the time, a song is closely associated with a particular artist (with "artist" including "bands"), which is not the case here, or if it is, then with the composer(s). Which of the allegedly nearly 30,000 versions should I choose, especially since, I admit, I don't know them all, haha!

The most recent version I'm aware of by Lana Del Rey is just as beautiful and relaxed as a warm summer day when nothing happens except for a deep sense of well-being and a few fluffy clouds in the blue sky, and I mean that in a positive sense. Janis Joplin also delivered a fantastic interpretation with Big Brother and the Holding Company, Love Sculpture (see their entry with another song) as well, and...

But "my" version is the rock-blues one by this Dutch band, which is highly recommended overall. The basic organ sound isn't majestically roaring but gritty-grinding, and the young Jan Akkerman showcases his guitar virtuosity in perfect combination with the pleasantly raspy voice of Kazimir Lux.

Rock-bluesy, yet still a relaxed summer day where more is happening musically. It will take me an eternity to get to know all the versions, but this one will always be among the best for eternity.

SUMMERTIME BLUES - EDDIE COCHRAN
(Jerry Capehart, Eddie Cochran)

I hear them calling – "Hey, why don't you pick the version by The Who, or Grand Funk Railroad, or, or, or...?" Not to mention the truly remarkable version by Rush.

Good question, simple answer: Because with so many fantastic versions, the choice is difficult, and this is meant to pay tribute to the artist who wrote this fundamentally awesome rock 'n' roll song, together with his manager – and also first released it.

His original, raw version still has a slight country feel, but it was already a strong piece for the time (1958), in every way. If I had heard it back then, I might have become a rock fan even earlier.

A bit Elvis-look-alike (he can't help it, and it doesn't hurt), Eddie Cochran also co-wrote many of his hits (including *Three Steps to Heaven*,

Somethin' Else, C'mon Everybody – both of the latter were quite "intense" for the time) and other songs. He was also a great guitarist of his time, possibly a co-inventor (which remains to be proven or disproven) of the "twang sound" attributed to Duane Eddy. At the very least, they knew and appreciated each other.

His voice could sound rough and rocky or gently Elvis-like, with all the nuances in between.

I actually considered using The Who's version here, or Grand Funk Railroad, or Rush, but The Who have so many incomparable original compositions that the selection is already huge and difficult enough. The live version by The Who is perhaps the most famous of this classic, and there's even a little-known studio version by them.

Summertime Blues is one of the most frequently covered rock 'n' roll songs of the 1950s, and rightly so! Even the Beach Boys contributed royalties to Eddie's coffers – or rather, to those of his estate administrators, because he sadly passed away much too early in 1960 due to a road accident in the UK.

I digress, but gladly – background information and all that.

With *Three Stars* (not composed by him), Eddie Cochran also paid tribute to Buddy Holly, the Big Bopper, and Ritchie Valens, although not as impressively as Mike Berry and the Outlaws did with their *Tribute to Buddy Holly* (see there), but it's noteworthy.

However, with **Summertime Blues**, he undoubtedly and very deservedly created his own monument for eternity!

THE AIR THAT I BREATHE - HOLLIES

(Hammond, Hazlewood))

The numerous fantastic hits by The Hollies are an incredibly important part of the "soundtrack" of the 1960s and the Beat explosion.

The Beat was there, but so was a very typical, unmistakably wonderful harmony singing, accompanied by wonderfully flowing melodies and great musical skill (not that I want to deny this to others, but The Hollies did loudly say "Here!" when this was being distributed). A vocal blueprint for later bands like the Eagles and many others, I claim.

They pressed their massive stamp mainly on compositions by others, but they could also put convincing notes to paper and into listeners' ears themselves.

They could handle the departure of their leading singers (Graham Nash in particular went on to have another very successful career – Allan Clarke also came back at one point) and always find appropriate "replacements," although this word does them injustice. With at least two original members, The Hollies still tour today, have never disbanded, and are one of the less than a handful of bands that have been continuously in existence for about 60 years, delighting the ears.

Absolutely outstanding "cinema" for your ears, and the elite gathered at the Abbey Road Studios, among them Alan Parsons as the sound engineer.

Many hits, many earworms... I'm torn between *He Ain't Heavy, He's My Brother*... and I choose **The Air That I Breathe**. By that time in the 1970s, quite different sounds were in demand, but timeless quality prevails.

The very first guitar tone gets under your skin, the following melting vocals even more, without being overly sentimental, a prime example of melody, of the air you need to breathe.

You want to breathe this enchanting air forever.

THE BLUEST BLUES - ALVIN LEE
(Alvin Lee)

What would the world, and especially music, be without the Blues? It would probably be quite "blue" – sad, downcast, miserable. The music of African American slaves who played and sang the Blues as a way to express their frustration, humiliation, and misery is the cornerstone of 20th-century music. Without the Blues, there would be no Rock 'n' Roll, no R 'n' B, no Beat, no Rock, no whatever.

Despite all the despondency, the Blues always conveys a certain hope not to be defeated. The gloomy mood is often projected onto the idea that a loved one has left. That's also the case in this Blues piece par excellence, even if it's "only blue-eyed Blues." But white musicians have amply demonstrated their ability to adapt this "black" music with almost as much, albeit somewhat different, fervor as black musicians.

As the frontman of the excellent Ten Years After, Alvin Lee was long regarded as one of the fastest guitarists in the world – well-known, but never in the big spotlight like Hendrix, Clapton, Beck, or Page, for example, although he had no need to hide from them. Well, nobody could really compete with Jimi.

After his departure from Ten Years After, Alvin released several excellent solo albums (including one in collaboration with Mylon LeFevre), and among them is *Nineteenninetyfour* with the overwhelming **The Bluest Blues**. Here, he proves, as if he needed to, that he was not only an outstanding guitarist in terms of speed but also a very sensitive one.

Following a brief, typical Blues intro and Alvin's earthy vocals (his loved one has left him), lightly underscored with an organ, the piece evolves into a Blues guitar orgy like no other, where Alvin pulls out all the stops, supported by George

Harrison on slide guitar (and his excellent band, of course, including Steve Gould, formerly of Rare Bird). This guitar, this sound, goes deep into your bones ("it cuts me like a knife," excerpt from the lyrics), and you can immerse yourself in this masterpiece for over 7 minutes, again and again, for all eternity.

Alvin Lee has already passed into eternity, but perhaps it's not black or brightly white but has the bluest blue you can hear, and Alvin plays along with it.

THE FINAL COUNTDOWN - EUROPE
(Joey Tempest)

Sweden has even more to offer musically than Harpo, if anyone still knows him, or Abba (with all due respect to their accomplishments) and the even better Roxette, at least for my ears, namely Europe.

Even though the Scandinavians always like to keep somewhat to themselves, almost all of them clearly identify with Europe, and that is what this hard rock/heavy metal group unequivocally represents with their name. Musically, they are not on the sidelines but right in the thick of things, having continued solidly with few lineup changes to this day, often offering solid, slightly symphonic heavy fare. And despite some English stage names, they are all "genuine Swedes," more or less.

More at home in the tradition of hard rock and sometimes labeled as "posers" by some "true metalheads," not least because of their then-stylized appearance, they landed a worldwide smash hit with **The Final Countdown** from their eponymous third album, which reached No. 1 in 25 countries! It was also a significant contribution and an important step in making the genre even more "respectable." Besides this mega-hit, I must admit I hardly know Europe, the band, and after streaming some of their music (which I rarely do and only for getting acquainted), I think I've opened up a new avenue for my collection. I am an ardent European anyway.

Beginning with muffled machine sounds (not in the shortened single version, if I'm not mistaken), a "fanfare choir" (it sounds like it, but it's keyboards) bursts forth, which would be well-suited to any historical film or symphony orchestra. A solid drum break, an emerging guitar riff, still underscored by these "fanfares," lead to the wonderfully clear, powerful vocals with their catchy chorus, then the great, intense-melodic guitar solo (a little reminiscent of Boston... oh, these comparisons always). Not quite worthy of the song's quality is the fade-out... out... out...

That's nitpicking at a high level, and what even defines a "song"? **The Final Countdown** is an anthem that is still sung worldwide, even in sports stadiums, although the lyrics are not meant to be sporty and are even inspired by David Bowie's *Space Oddity* (with its own entry in this book). "We're leaving together, heading for Venus..." is a rough summary.

But a final countdown always fits well, especially in our time, before eternity soon arrives with blaring fanfares and crashing guitars.

THE NIGHT WE DRANK THE STARS - DAVE EVANS & NITZINGER

(John Nitzinger)

This dramatic piece almost convinces me to switch from being a dedicated beer enthusiast to joining the ranks of champagne drinkers, as it tells the fictional story of the invention of this sparkling beverage in an immensely impressive way.

The album *Revenge* (2013), from which this song comes, is a masterpiece of exceptional quality, and I must and will hereby set a milestone for it, somewhat apart from the actual intention of this book (that gives me an idea...). A masterpiece with a particularly stupid cover, but the songs more than convince and compensate for it. Revenge, for what, and why? Perhaps because earlier works of these two top musicians did not receive the recognition they deserved? Possibly, and if so, the revenge has been extremely effective and, in a figurative sense, bloodthirsty successful.

Dave Evans was fired as the first singer of AC/DC after their first single, and John Nitzinger did not achieve the resounding success with his group of the same (sur)name (and only a few fine hard rock albums that should definitely be reissued). For a long time, little to nothing was heard from both, with occasional, largely unnoticed exceptions or as backing musicians (but who pays attention to those anyway?).

Only from the 2000s did both apparently reassert themselves and become more active, then joining forces for this monster album. Dave's powerful, forceful voice doesn't quite have the screaming factor of Bon Scott or Brian Johnson, but can at least fully convince here, and John's sawing, screeching, grinding, tearing guitar is a pleasure beyond compare, although in this song it takes a back seat in favor of slightly quieter passages, fortunately only slightly. That's why I almost chose the song *Going Back to Texas* from this album, where John's guitar really pulls the last nails out of the wall.

Revenge is the perfect synthesis of rock, hard rock, rock 'n' roll, and metal, the essence. Island question – if I could only take one single ROCK album, it could be this one. But the rock would possibly shatter the island.

Alright, **The Night We Drank The Stars** is the chosen song, not least because of its drama and the dynamics that I love so much. A toast to this song and the album, with champagne or beer, definitely not sparkling water – we will drink these stars for all eternity!

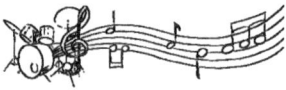

THE SOUND OF SILENCE - SIMON & GARFUNKEL

(Paul Simon)

"Sweeter the bells never ring" ... or something like that. When these sweet, heavenly tones broke into the emerging post-beat and pre-rock era in 1965, it was already a surprise, but one that you couldn't resist. The starting shot (haha, given the title) of an international mega-career, not a "beat group" but a duo, visually unassuming, apart from (Art) Garfunkel's unruly hair. People might have made fun of the name (Simon and Furunkel), and at least here in Germany, hardly anyone initially knew that these were the surnames of the artists and not their first names (as it could have been Tom & Jerry, their previous duo name – like cat and mouse, that's how they behaved before and after their later separation).

Even the name of the song is genius – **The Sound of Silence**. Truly heavenly harmony singing with airy swinging guitars, underpinned with a certain beat – it hits you right in the soul. Further great hits followed (*Bridge Over Troubled Water, Mrs.*

Robinson – a great soundtrack for the great film *The Graduate* – *The Boxer*, among others), but by then you were already familiar with this fabulous sound, and while the element of surprise from **The Sound of Silence** was no longer there, it was always welcome.

With their golden voices, Simon & Garfunkel could make almost any song special, even if a composition itself might not have been that great. On their first, still fairly unsuccessful album, it was called *The Sounds of Silence*, and the song was subsequently reworked with a bit of electric guitar and drums, then titled **The Sound of Silence** – the rest is history. The hit version without the "s" then appeared on the second album, which was titled *Sounds of Silence*. That's something somebody may understand... but you don't have to.

Cover versions are doomed to fail – even if relatively recently such a version was high in the charts, probably owed to the class of the song. Was that by Disturbed? Seems so, from what I looked up – absolutely terrible, an outstanding song apparently can't be completely ruined by something like that. I listened briefly – very briefly, it's really awful, just disturbed. But it seems to be what I mean. The name fits. I don't listen to much radio, and whenever this violation of the piece was played, I quickly switched it off.

The original tone (or sound, noise, etc.) of silence echoes forever.

THE VALENTYNE SUITE - COLOSSEUM
(Colosseum)

Not a song in the traditional sense, as there is no singing here, apart from occasional elegiac background vocals.

Referred to as *Valentine Suite* on a compilation, this more than 16-minute-long piece, named after the album of the same name (LP, as it was called back then), is an unprecedentedly dynamic, melodious, and rocking masterpiece. Each instrument gets its solo performances, driven by the genius drummer Jon Hiseman, one of the all-time best in his field. You can bathe in the guitar solo, and in this context, the saxophone is also a welcome rock instrument (as in some other cases). While its master, Dick Heckstall-Smith, was a well-known luminary in the field, one wonders why the guitarist James Litherland did not achieve higher honors. The composer credits vary, with individual parts sometimes attributed to specific musicians, but the entire group is also listed.

A lesson in terms of "dynamics," it is almost blasphemous to try to describe this hammer instrumental piece, divided into three thematic cycles, full of wonderful melodies, gently flowing transitions, and fiercely rocking passages with words. Even after more than 50 years, it hasn't gathered any dust, and you should close your eyes, turn the headphones up LOUD, and dive into the eternally fantastic sonic spheres of **The Valentyne Suite**.

TIME HAS COME TODAY - CHAMBERS BROTHERS

(Willie Chambers, Joseph Chambers)

Tick.... Tock.... Tick.... Tock.... Tick.... Tock.... Tick.... Tock.... TickTock TickTock, TickTockTickTockTickTock...

The introductory percussion beats simulate the clock, which speeds up more and more before the other instruments and the soul-infused, excellent vocals kick in, offering a great, hypnotic mix that slows down again towards the middle of the song, almost silent, before starting again – finest Soul-Psychedelic-Flower-Power-Rock!

Let me simplify things and cite the back cover text of the CD of the first album of these four African American (real) brothers with their white drummer, a certain provocation and statement at that time in the still racially charged USA (unfortunately until today) (just like the Equals in the UK with a different kind of music, great in their own way).

"With Gospel roots woven between rock and soul, wrapped in a grand cloak of psychedelic music, the Chambers Brothers proved to be one of the truly innovative and provocative bands of the late 1960s."

That sums it up. *People Get Ready* or *New Generation*, just to name two, are further examples of their excellent songs, but the 11-minute **Time Has Come Today** is their masterpiece, which was also a big hit in a shortened single version.

I was fortunate enough to see the Chambers Brothers live in London in 1968, with a fantastic light show, bubbling, swirling colourful bubbles, etc., as was customary at the time. Various scents wafted around too – but their wonderful performance and the I-don't-know-how-long live version of this hypnotic track were enough to experience a first-rate Flower Power sensory trip.

The mentioned single version is not bad either, there are even several slightly different ones, but the full-length album version is unbeatable and indisputable.

To anyone who doesn't know this piece, I can say only: "The time has come" to make up for this omission. Today and for eternity, time always comes and goes, but this anthem will never fade.

TIME SELLER - SPENCER DAVIS GROUP

(Davis, Hardin)

With the name of this band, surely everyone would have expected me to mention one of their big hits, especially the bold first one, *Keep On Running*, or *Somebody Help Me*, *Gimme Some Lovin'*, or *I'm A Man* (see Chicago Transit Authority), and these songs all deserved it, no doubt.

But I deliberately chose this great piece because a) it is less known and b) in my opinion, it is at least equally top-class.

I was very disappointed at that time that this powerful number only made it to number 30 in the UK charts, and the successor *Mr. Second Class* didn't even achieve that, although by no means second-class.

After the departure of Steve and Muff Winwood, the Spencer Davis Group presented themselves with the album *With Their New Face On*, with precisely that, a new face, or rather two new faces: Eddie Hardin and Phil Sawyer were more than mere "replacements" for the Winwood brothers.

The almost continuous strong riff from beginning to end drills into the ears, and one might think that violins, violas, or similar instruments are responsible for it, but I cannot find any confirmation of that. In any case, it rocks heavily, and the man whose job it is to sell time does this with great success – selling to eternity!

Just listen! A more than successful slight deviation from the earthy R & B sound with an equally successful slight turn towards earthy, slightly psychedelic realms.

By the way, the track *Don't Want You No More* from the same album was covered by the Allman Brothers Band on their first album. Absolutely top class, like everything from the Allman Brothers Band (with their own entry), but the Spencer Davis Group's original can of course be more than well enjoyed.

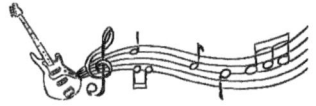

TRIBUTE TO BUDDY HOLLY –
MIKE BERRY AND THE OUTLAWS
(Geoff Goddard)

When I first heard this song, its atmosphere with its airy, resonant guitar sound (reminiscent of the Shadows, who I discovered a bit later) and rolling drums immediately captivated me. Although I didn't quite understand what it was about at the time, it was clear to me that it was about a tragic event.

I don't know when I first heard it, probably quite a while later, after it was a hit in the UK (1961). Not a huge hit, probably because the BBC had banned the song due to its "morbid" content (as I only recently found out).

In 1959, Buddy Holly, Richie Valens, and "The Big Bopper" died in a plane crash; there is much to read and find about the details (largely known to music fans), and I don't want to elaborate on them here. Above all, Buddy Holly's influence on the music world, not least on the Beatles, cannot be underestimated.

Not a massive hit, but a truly great song from the English hit factory of producer Joe Meek. Despite many singles and his equally successful "re-make" of this song in 1975, Mike Berry has not left a big mark, not even as an actor, which was his second later profession, so to speak. I don't mean any harm to him, quite the opposite. And it would certainly be unfair to say that he wanted to "profit" from this tragedy, especially since he didn't write the song himself. These "Outlaws" have nothing to do with the ones listed elsewhere.

A song that brings tears to the eyes, not written by Mike Berry himself, but beautifully and poignantly interpreted by him and his colleagues. While Buddy Holly and his unfortunate companions have long been resting in the eternal musical grounds, this serves as a very thoughtful and memorable tribute to him for eternity, in addition to his own songs, interpreted by himself (and by many others).

UNCHAINED MELODY -
RIGHTEOUS BROTHERS

(Alex North, Hy Zaret)

My keyboard is somehow so greasy... oh, that's the grease oozing out of it. But it feels good.

In the middle of the most musically innovative decade of all time, amidst bubbling beat, pop, and rock sounds, came this splendid tearjerker from the American duo, after they split from their group The Paramours. As an echo from earlier times, there were also some other "tatters" that die-hard beat and pop fans just wrinkled their noses at, but I mean, that wasn't the case here, at least not for me. Because this sound, this melody, this voice just got under your skin and straight into your soul, whether you wanted it or not, pure goosebumps and "schmaltz" put aside.

The Righteous Brothers had already set the tone with *You've Lost That Lovin' Feelin'* and had also attracted attention on this side of the pond, with further hits to follow. The influence of producer Phil Spector is audible, albeit not as prominent as with many other "Spector Sounds." Phil Spector is a chapter of his own and should not be further considered here, that would be too much. At that time, he used to put his "junk productions" on the B-side of singles, as he did with this one, and called the radio DJs across the country not to play this side, after more and more ignored the A-side (*Hung on You*) and instead sent **Unchained**

Melody over the airwaves. There are, however, different versions regarding the actual producer.

I've always wondered why this poignant heartache-longing-love ballad, with its "blue-eyed-soul" voice that almost spills over and reaches unexpected heights, and whose melody oils the ear canals so uniquely, is "unchained," but it's never been questioned. So I have to do some research now...

...and I stumbled upon some surprising facts. Originally stemming from a prison film in 1955 ("Unchained," ah-ha...), **Unchained Melody** is one of the most covered songs of the last century (like some others in this book) and is the only song that has conquered the UK charts with four different versions, into the 21st century! One never stops learning... The film was probably not a big hit, but this recording by the Righteous Brothers was all the more so, with swooning violins and all that jazz, a real blockbuster, so to speak.

And it is generally recognized that the Righteous Brothers made this "their song", and whoever surrenders to this **Unchained Melody** has their incomparable version in their ears for all eternity, where there are no chains, but only this ooooh so beautiful melody.

WE ARE THE CHAMPIONS - QUEEN

(Freddie Mercury)

Everyone knows Queen, not just the Queen of the United Kingdom of Great Britain (sadly demised by now, and I'm far from being a royalist, but think nobody could help but like and admire the Queen).

Strangely, I'm also not the biggest Queen fan – I can't really explain why. I appreciate them, and they have delivered many great songs, no doubt. They have been and are a big name in the rock and show business with an unmistakable, absolutely unique style. In contrast to many other artists, whose entire works I own (or at least almost completely and/or still working on), I only have a meager two CDs from Queen, Greatest Hits I and II. Not that the CDs are meager, but the quantity. But they still offer me more than 30 of their, I repeat, great songs, which still belong to the standard repertoire of almost every radio station. I used to have a few of their regular albums on vinyl.

Some readers would surely have expected *Bohemian Rhapsody* here, or *We Will Rock You*, or... the options are numerous.

But I specifically chose **We Are The Champions** because this hit is probably the most played song by Queen worldwide (I haven't researched), as it is repeatedly used on many occasions, especially at major sporting events, where it fits perfectly. It

will presumably remain so for a long time, securing a well-deserved place "for eternity."
I don't need to say anything about the song itself; everyone really knows it, and that's a well deserved, good thing.

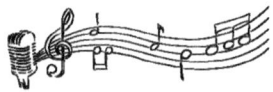

WHEEL IN THE SKY - JOURNEY

(Schon, Fleischman, D. Valory)

Journey have had a long, diverse, and highly productive journey and are still on the road, which particularly delights me as their enthusiastic fan from the very beginning until today.

Founded by ex-Santana members (notably the excellent guitarist Neil Schon as the sole permanent member and head of the group) and other outstanding musicians, the British multi-talented drummer Aynsley Dunbar joined soon, even before the first album was recorded, one of the best in his field. He is also known to be one of the most challenging in terms of collaboration, as he admits himself. Previously the successor to Ringo in Rory Storm & the Hurricanes, after he was recruited by the Beatles for a global career (also one of the best overall, often scorned by people who have no idea about drumming), he has probably played in more bands and projects than any other drummer (Carmine Appice could be a contender). Besides those mentioned above, I won't even begin to list others; it would probably be easier to name the bands he hasn't played with. I digress, but that is also a concern of this book and fits perfectly here, Journey...

Their first three excellent albums went largely unnoticed – mostly instrumental, they offered wonderful sounds that still bore traces of their Santana origins, intertwined with powerful rock and light forays into the jazz-rock and prog-rock corners.

A turning point in their journey was the emergence and entry of singer Steve Perry with his impressive, relatively high, and hauntingly pleasant voice, which could sound both rocky and sentimental with all the nuances in between. The sound became more bombastic, and the first album with Steve Perry was a commercially successful big hit, followed by many more even greater successes. It was called *Infinity* – *Infinity*, eternity, the name is a sign. But it was the end of Aynsley as Journey's drummer.

All the songs on this album are fascinatingly great, but perhaps **Wheel in the Sky** stands out a bit. A perfect mix of gentle keyboard intros, powerful guitars, Steve's extraordinary vocals, and great solos, with melody always at the forefront. The **Wheel in the Sky** keeps turning forever, and the journey continues. Various lineup changes did not diminish their increasing success with even more bombast; Journey became one of THE live arena attractions, especially in the United States, but their albums also sold extremely well worldwide and are among the top sellers overall.

The journey continues, even after a hiatus from the late 1980s to the mid-1990s. Their current Filipino singer, Arnel Pineda, hardly makes one miss Steve Perry, Neil Schon sets the direction and tones down the bombast for the sake of his "axe," ensuring that the wheel in the sky keeps turning in the right direction.

(Their own, closely faithful remake from 2008 – with Arnel, on the 2-CD album *Revelation* – is no less impressive, although the original may have a slight edge simply because one/I have heard it a hundred times and know every note by heart, twice.)

WHEN A MAN LOVES A WOMAN – PERCY SLEDGE

(Lewis, Wright)

Soul music is sparsely represented in this book, I must admit, yet it has so much soul and has produced as many great artists as almost any other (fairly) clearly defined genre, except for the blues, with which it is, of course, related (as is almost every other genre – rock 'n' roll, rock, hard rock, R&B, even the beat, and so on).

I do appreciate soul music, but I am generally inclined toward the somewhat different "heavy" side, which could serve as an explanation for myself.

Otis Redding, Aretha Franklin, Wilson Pickett, or the Four Tops, Supremes, Temptations, or Marvin Gaye from the "soul offshoot" Tamla Motown, to name just a few, are just the tiny tip of the black iceberg – Black people, generally speaking, can sing better than White people. That's my opinion.

[Is that racist, is it expressed incorrectly? I have been vilified and defamed on the internet by idiots who cannot read and understand, even for other clearly anti-racist, harmless statements. I am so anti-racist and anti-fascist; you can't look any further to the left. I think, and hope, that most true music lovers and connoisseurs are not idiots. This off-topic digression is on my mind right now; I ask for your understanding – old news by the time this book is printed. But when it comes to liestening to soul music, you can drink both hot and cold coffee, if you know what I mean.]

In the 1960s, the new soul music, which was new to local ears, enriched the pop, beat, and rock-oriented charts with its new sounds and great hits. The vocals and rhythm immediately seep into the bloodstream, and the frequent blend with gospel singing can quickly feel ecstatic. Percy Sledge, on the other hand, topped the charts on both sides of the Atlantic with his slow, organ-dominated love ballad that melts every heart. If not, you don't have one.

More than the organ, Percy's devoted voice dominates this enchanting melody and brought the Atlantic label its first gold record. His first and biggest hit was not his only one and has often been covered, but no cover reaches this overwhelming intensity.

When a Man Loves a Woman... then the heart beats, time stands still, and eternity has begun.

WHEN DEATH CALLS - BLACK SABBATH
(Black Sabbath)
When thinking of Black Sabbath, almost everyone would immediately think of Ozzy Osbourne and *Paranoid*, but there was a life after Ozzy, and how! For me, by far the best Black Sabbath album is *Headless Cross* (also a great song, like every track on this particularly strong piece of plastic) with singer Tony Martin, who, in my opinion, can certainly hold his own against Ozzy, although perhaps lacking that certain, small Ozzy touch.

The standout song on this overall more than remarkable album (with Cozy Powell on drums) is **When Death Calls**, not only because of its lyrics. Its gentle intro leads with the dynamics I love so much to the hard riffs of the incomparable Tony Iommi (he is Mr. Black Sabbath himself, not Ozzy), then fades away again, builds up – just dynamics in the best sense. Tony's (Martin) singing and screams cut through bone and marrow, and the entire enormous force, coupled with melody and, not least, these lyrics, makes all the hair stand on end!

Such a short article about such a gigantic song (and a giant group)... but one simply has to listen, and as mentioned at the beginning, the length of an article has nothing to do with the quality of the song. No one can escape the call of death.

One of a handful of songs that should be played at my funeral – for the journey into eternity. Whether I will live to experience that...

WHEN EVENING COMES -
KEN HENSLEY

(Ken Hensley)

Ken who? This Ken, exactly. Multi-instrumentalist, genius, significant part of the early Uriah Heep (see there) as a musician and composer, he had already demonstrated his skills beforehand. Without him, their career might have taken a different path, not to detract from the others. They have proven their competence and class to the fullest extent in changing lineups up to the present day. Uriah Heep without Ken Hensley is possible, but the reverse is also true. And *From Time to Time* (another one of his wonderful songs), he has also mixed it up with his old buddies; old love never rusts.

This track from his first solo album immediately knocks your socks off, or rather the guitar with its pulling, yearning, melancholic sound, along with Ken's wonderfully catchy vocals – a rock ballad that crawls deep under your skin and makes it tingle.

Ken was primarily the keyboardist in Uriah Heep, but his solo works also prove that he excels at everything else just as well. Apart from drums (which he can also play), he often plays everything himself on his first solo album and later, he's also a gifted singer. He manages, in a magical way or however else, to convey the heavy/hard rock sound without presenting heavy/hard rock, with wonderful ballads or rather gentle rockers prevailing – with occasional exceptions that confirm the rule, for example, with his later Scandinavian band Live Fire, but always with that special Ken Hensley touch.

Melody coupled with hard rock sound is Ken's strength, among many others – he has worked with countless other luminaries, and countless other luminaries call on him when they need someone who "has got it." His solo works are excellent and manageable, somewhat convoluted with various compilations, his work in the "background" is almost immeasurable. He not only creates and writes charismatic songs but also looks the part with his long hair (always good!)

and a slightly weathered face like a "Native American" (though he is not) – I could kiss him (and some other musicians) although I am definitely not gay. His business qualities seem to be diametrically opposed to his musical ones, or perhaps he is not interested in them at all...

That is the problem – he and his wonderful work are far too little recognized. But I reckon he can live with that as long as he himself and other musicians appreciate what he is worth. Ken Hensley is a great one, a star in the music sky that will not burn out for eternity, especially not as evening approaches.

[Tears are flowing now, truly and once again – just before the first publication of this book, Ken passed away. His star is now high in the sky.]

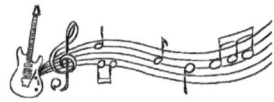

WHISKEY IN THE JAR - THIN LIZZY
(Traditional)

At some point in the early 1970s, I heard and saw an unknown band in some London basement venue – Thin Lizzy, never heard before, but impressive, with that black singer and bassist with a Hendrix mane, clearly the leader of the gang. An Irishman, as I later learned, and so to speak, Mr. Thin Lizzy himself. (According to Wikipedia, the "first successful black Irishman in the music business.")

He composed most of their songs, but not this one. With origins in the 17th century, the Irish pub and drinking song is the oldest song mentioned in this book, even though it may have sounded somewhat different at that time.

Often covered (Dubliners, Pogues, Metallica, and so on), but it was Thin Lizzy who brought whiskey to the charts with their wonderfully rocking version of **Whiskey in the Jar** and made it unforgettable. The band and their boss, Phil Lynott, were not initially pleased with the release because it "didn't represent their style." Fortunately, they were mistaken. They were the ones who infused this heavenly "fine beer" beverage with its characteristic smoky-soft-scratchy musical soul.

The rich guitar intro goes down like a good whiskey, and that delightful guitar sound accompanies almost the entire piece with its irresistible melody, alternating with Phil's powerful voice, almost like a second voice, both underscored with a slightly "fiddly," presumably acoustic guitar, like a fiddle. There's a great guitar solo on top, and perceptibly/audibly, the guitar anticipates the later-adopted "twin-guitar sound" by Thin Lizzy (see Wishbone Ash and others). Phil's strong vocals and the driving rhythm make not just the intro but the entire song flow through the ears like good Irish whiskey down the throat – it's something to savor!

Thin Lizzy could (and did) get heavier, but they were primarily always more on the second front, as were the excellent guitarists who passed through the band, of whom, other than Gary Moore, none achieved great breakthroughs but were highly regarded and continue to be by fans.

Cited as an influence by many rock/hard rock bands, with Phil's early death in 1986, the group's work and thus many possible great songs came to a sad end. The group continued for a while, not bad, but without Phil, it was more like a jug without or with only a little whiskey inside.

However, this and the songs created during his lifetime continue, and similar to how The Animals made the traditional song *The House of the Rising Sun* (see there) "their" song, Thin Lizzy did the same with **Whiskey in the Jar**. Even though Metallica celebrate the whiskey in their own way, they clearly orient themselves to Thin Lizzy's version.

If whiskey is drunk in eternity, then this version of the song plays – if not, one can do without this version of eternity.

WHITE ROOM - CREAM
(Jack Bruce, Pete Brown)
Hmm, first class whipped cream! Cream, you don't really need to say much about them, but a

few lines it shall be. These three exceptional musicians, or Cream, are generally regarded as the first supergroup, even though at the time of the trio's formation, they weren't really in the focus of the broader pop and beat audience, but were highly, no, most highly esteemed by their fellow musicians. With Cream, that changed, and Clapton, Bruce, and Baker became known to the "ordinary fan" as true masters of their respective crafts and superheroes.

After a slightly more pop-oriented start with still unusual songs at the time (*Wrapping Paper* or *I Feel Free*), they soon found their own style. This mixture of blues and rock, mostly at a slow tempo with jazz and psychedelic elements, has no precedent and no real imitators – simply Cream, done, unique, and unmatched.

All these elements can of course be found in **White Room**, not least the psychedelic, twisted text, and I have often wondered how that introductory, beautifully haunting floating tone came about. Slightly underlaid by Ginger's drums before he and Bruce really kick in. Guitar... yes and no, and I suspect it's a blend of Eric's guitar and Felix Pappalardi's viola, who not only produced the *Wheels of Fire* album but also occasionally played this violin-like instrument. That "haunting sound" comes back later, along with Eric's wah-wah guitar and his skills, of course. Incidentally, this was the first double album ever to achieve platinum status – times were changing, as was the music and the media: albums were in demand, breaking the sole focus on singles.

Back in the day, a "standard" at every hippie party, perhaps some intoxication enjoyed there led to another **White Room**, but even without drugs, one can linger excellently in this **White Room**, and that for eternity, amen.

WITH A LITTLE HELP FROM MY FRIENDS - JOE COCKER

(Lennon, McCartney)

Cover versions are usually just that and rarely earn my approval. But in this book they are impossible to avoid, especially when it comes to the Beatles. And cover versions can be fantastic when completely revamped and reinterpreted (see, among others, Rod Stewart).

Joe Cocker's first attempt with a Beatles coversong *I'll Cry Instead* was a cover that deserved the name, attracting attention only to his voice, nothing more, if at all. *Marjorine* (co-written by him and no Beatles involved) fared somewhat better, but then **With a Little Help from My Friends** stormed the still heavily pop-oriented charts in 1968, and Joe managed to make this song his own.

The soft organ intro, then powerful drums, Jimmy Page's wonderfully "pulling" guitar (in this case confirmed and not a rumor), bass, and Joe's incomparable voice, in alternating vocals with a glorious female choir, up to his mighty primal scream, transform this piece with its dragging tempo into something new, completely different from the slightly faster original version delivered by Ringo in a sing-along style (and fitting perfectly into the concept of the century's masterpiece *Sgt. Pepper's Lonely Hearts Club Band*).

Here, however, the concept is only the primal force of Joe Cocker that brought him the definitive breakthrough with his performance of "his" song at the Woodstock Festival (without Jimmy Page).

With his talent to make every song "his" song even without great compositional skills, Joe Cocker has particularly qualified for eternity with this, with a little help from his friends.

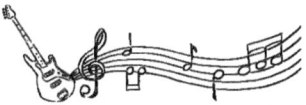

WON'T GET FOOLED AGAIN - THE WHO
(Pete Townshend)
Who? Oh, the who... to say much more about these icons here would be like carrying owls to Athens.

Even if I repeat myself (as I have repeated several times) – in hardly any entry in this book did the choice of the song give me as much trouble as in this case, perhaps even as difficult as in no other case. (And since this book is hardly read all at once, the final order is different from what it is now when I am writing, such repetitions are not so noticeable, I hope ... and so be it.)

The Who have so many pieces that have lodged themselves in the brains of many listeners for eternity ... oh man, which one should I choose? *I Can't Explain* (their first single under this name and a big hit right away), *My Generation, Substitute, Pinball Wizard, Magic Bus* – that should be enough here, the list would otherwise be too long.

Their initial image as rough rascals suited them in a way, but was also contradictory to their lyrics. Smashing their instruments (guitar and drums) after (almost) every performance quickly became their trademark, but so did the lyrics with socio-political content – the perplexity and criticism of youth towards existing conditions.

The brute guitar sound later gave way to a somewhat softer tone, without ever disappearing completely. Their overall sound was and is unique. Pete Townshend is not the great guitar soloist but shapes the sound with his blend of rhythm and lead guitar, and of course with the compositions mostly stemming from his pen.

The Who are also the only group without voluntary lineup changes, one could also say, without any lineup changes. Only death could part them. And along with the Rolling Stones (still roughly in their original lineup), the Who are one of the two surviving groups from the "prehistoric" era of the Beat era (excluding the still touring Hollies with almost an entirely different lineup). I'm getting into a ramble, but the Who deserve it, if one sees my rambling in a positive light.

Some may protest now, saying Kenny Jones came in for the late Keith Moon – but not really as a "member," even though he was there for a long time. At some point, he left the club again; he was just a longer-term (excellent) "substitute," never a true member of the band, like no other of the numerous musicians with whom the Who have worked in the studio and especially on tours until today. They simply became fewer and Pete and Roger (and John, as long as he lived) got whoever they needed. And whoever was brought in could and can be proud to work or have worked with one of the best bands in the world.

Oh, I realize this might be the longest entry in this book. Well, one will be the longest, and in terms of the artist, I have pondered the longest for this song, so it fits.

After experiencing the Who live for the first time in 1965, I was bitterly disappointed. After a few support acts (which I have forgotten), they finally took the stage after an agonizingly long wait, played utter crap for about 15 minutes, and smashed their guitar and drums, and that was it. "Never again," I thought – I later witnessed some absolutely great concerts of theirs, with and without wreckage and with and without Keith Moon.

About the song. **Won't Get Fooled Again** is the essence that captures and expands the Who's essence. Brute guitar sound, as always, or often, Roger's inimitable vocals, melody and structure despite all the force, and the consistent pulsating synthesizer is the expansion. By now, the reader should listen to this masterpiece. The lyrics can be interpreted one way or another – "the same shit everywhere, but we won't let ourselves be fooled" is one possibility, to put it succinctly. The only proper "solo" is reserved for the synthesizer towards the end, a quiet, extended passage before Roger heralds, no, shouts in the still crashing ending with one of the best YEAH! screams of all time. This scream melts the spine and echoes into eternity, not just in my mind.

When you're writing, you're researching too, at least occasionally – **Won't Get Fooled Again** was the last song Keith Moon played live, I did not know that until now. Before he allowed himself to be fooled, he passed the drumsticks, no, the spoon.

A "secret" fifth member of the Who, in this sense, and a friend, since the 70s was the "guitar wizard" and roadie Alan Rogan (who also worked for

George Harrison, AC/DC, Eric Clapton, and other luminaries). Broken guitar (Pete sometimes let it remain somewhat intact), guitar problems, which guitar to take – Alan was there with advice and assistance, besides moonlighting as a musician himself. Just before I could meet him as planned and hoped in 2019, I was very eager to hear many exciting stories, he unfortunately died of his cancer. Obituaries in the New York Times and the Times, on the Who website, and elsewhere testify to the significance of this "star of the stars." I am proud to now own two of his personally worn T-shirts – all of this is a very special story.

OK, this will probably be the longest post (and it has remained so). **Won't Get Fooled Again** is also available as a single version, but I strongly recommend the more than 8-minute version from the album *Who's Next*. I probably don't need to mention that it's great overall, but the cover also deserves special attention. Four "rascals" (the Who, who else?) have just urinated on a huge monument, not unlike the one from the epic film *2001: A Space Odyssey*.

Typical Who – not pissed off, ah, wrong, unsurpassed, provocative, questioning. With *Tommy*, they may have created the first "rock opera," the scholars are not entirely sure (definitely the most successful) and were initially considered "Mods," but one could also describe them as the first punks in every respect. Now I have carried many owls to Athens, but perhaps also some that not everyone knew.

Anyway, I won't be fooled, not yesterday, not today, and not for eternity.

YOU KEEP ME HANGIN' ON - ROD STEWART

(Holland, Dozier, Holland)

No, not *Sailing* or any of his other great hits, but for me, this album track is the standout song by Rod among many other outstanding ones.

Everyone knows Rod Stewart, even the younger generation, and opinions about him are divided. His detractors call him a "poser" or say "all his songs sound the same," while his fans call him an artist and singer of the highest caliber. Either you hate him or you love him. I love him to a great extent, I'm not gay (and neither is he), and I'm not a woman who loves him particularly (though many women do). Women usually have better taste.

He sounds the same all the time – well, superficially that might be true, but his charismatic, exceptionally smooth yet rough voice is presented with many nuances that leave his stamp on each song, you just have to listen. Even from a bad song, he still makes at least a decent or even a good one. And in that sense, no, "always the same" is also good – you know what to expect and look forward to it.

Rod Stewart is also a decent composer when he puts some effort into it here and there – but his talent is his throat and the ability to always gather the best musicians around him and make something special out of every song. And these best musicians must have their reasons for gathering around him – not just with regard to their bank account.

Originally a great hit for the Supremes, Rod and his fellow musicians deconstruct this great Tamla Motown song, mix everything up, and put it back together. This is not a simple "cover song," this is a new piece of music based on another, that's what an interpretation is all about.

The wonderful, tame organ intro with the then powerful drums and Jim Cregan's guitar that takes your shoes off until Rod finally lets his vocal instrument come into play – an aural delight like no other and another lesson in dynamics (sorry, I just can't think of a better word for it). A (very) restrained middle section (dynamics, did I mention that already?), then again that incomparable guitar, and Rod's voice... for more than 7 minutes, you can bathe in this sound painting. (Also noteworthy is the psychedelic, completely different version of this song by Vanilla Fudge.)

I wanted to present songs here, also with occasional references to albums. This is an opportunity – the album *Foot Loose & Fancy Free* is for me THE Rod Stewart album (I have them all) ever, not just because of **You Keep Me Hangin' On**. His heart-wrenching interpretations of *(If Loving You Is Wrong) I Don't Want To Be Right* or *I Was Only Joking* are simply... heart-wrenching. The whole album is one of the best for eternity.

Enough of the praise – a reliable companion for over 50 years (earliest beginnings with the Jeff Beck Group), Rod Stewart never keeps me hangin' on, and his enthusiasm for football (the real thing) and model trains makes him all the more likable.

Not a letdown, but a perennial burning flame par excellence.

YOU'LL NEVER WALK ALONE – GERRY & THE PACEMAKERS

(Rodgers, Hammerstein)

Another one of those common songs that might make some readers sigh.

As an archetype of the Mersey sound, perhaps even more so than the Beatles, who initiated it and then... became the Beatles, Gerry Marsden, with his slightly sentimental voice and his band, imprinted this American musical song from 1945 into the world's memory and transformed it.

Their *Ferry 'cross the Mersey* is a wonderful Mersey hit, but **You'll Never Walk Alone** by Gerry & The Pacemakers is an incomparable worldwide hit and has become THE football anthem everywhere on the globe.

Not only for BvB (Borussia Dortmund), but also occasionally for VfL Bochum, and always somewhere in some stadium. And decades later, I had the honor of experiencing it live, emanating from thousands of throats at Anfield Road with FC Liverpool – pure goosebumps! And which other club could have founded this tradition?

I don't need to say more about it – Rockers and Soccers: **You'll Never Walk Alone!**

YOU REALLY GOT ME - THE KINKS
(Ray Davies)

After two unsuccessful attempts by the Kinks, **You Really Got Me** burst into the largely tame charts in 1964, swiftly claiming the No. 1 spot in the UK. With its powerful guitar riff, this track is widely considered the birth of "Heavy Metal", despite the term itself emerging much later. Sure, this is disptuable. [And this is the first entry I wrote and now the last one in this book – if anyone is interested. The reverse is not true.]

At that time, it was not uncommon for skilled studio musicians to record a song, which was then attributed to a group that often had to diligently learn it to deliver a passable performance in their increasingly frequent live shows.

For a long time, a rumor persisted that Jimmy Page (Yardbirds, Led Zeppelin) played the solo in **You Really Got Me**. Many sources have debunked this, not least of all Jimmy Page himself. Notably, Ray Davies claimed in his autobiography (1998) that he shouted "fuck off!" to his brother Dave to ensure he wouldn't miss the cue for the solo, and that this can be "clearly" heard (especially on the CD), although he later shouted "Oh no!" over the drum break preceding the solo to mask it.

I've tried to listen to it, in both the mono and stereo versions, repeatedly, but in vain. Perhaps others have better ears than I do and are as keen-eared as Ray.

Nevertheless, this "Song of the Century" meant "fuck off!" (get going!) for the Kinks' journey to many more, mostly more laid-back, wonderful hits (*Sunny Afternoon, Waterloo Sunset* are just a few of them), even if they initially only "copied" this success formula with their follow-up hit *All Day And All Of The Night.*

Mastermind Ray Davies is one of the truly great songwriters, and the Kinks are one of the foundational pillars upholding the rock sky.

Rarely covered (among others by Van Halen), the instrumental version (!) by Mott the Hoople (see there) on their debut album five years later (1969) is all the more remarkable and even closer to the concept of "Heavy Metal." This ingenious riff grips you, nomen est omen, and never lets go into eternity. Best in the original, unsurpassed!

AFTERWORD

Fettich (meaning "all done"), as we say here in the Ruhrgebiet (Ruhr Area), and the final entry fits quite well, coincidentally following alphabetical sorting. These 100 songs have brought me much joy and will continue to do so forever, as well as some head-scratching in terms of the overall and specific selection. But such contemplation has been and was enjoyable. I've recalled many things and learned some new ones as well.

I can't ignore the twinge of guilt that comes with it, though. There are so many great songs and outstanding artists that could have been included or at least mentioned, but 100 is 100, end of story. Some had to be left behind, unfortunately. My potential list is much (much, much) longer, and at another time, it could have been this or that song and/or artist instead of this or that. I won't even begin to list which ones.

I wrote in a jumble, as things came to mind and to my ears, but with the final alphabetical sorting, some "funny" constellations emerged.

I won't have enough material in my list for another 100 songs (absolute TOP songs in my estimation), and even though there are hundreds, thousands of songs that I like very very much, very much, much or really enjoy listening to, they differ from those that go deep, very deep under my skin, to the core. Strangely, there are artists like Joe Bonamassa, whom I can listen to devotedly for hours and whom I appreciate to (almost) no end... but a specific song of his hasn't firmly ingrained itself in me.

A special thanks to my friend and wonderful graphic designer, Marco, in distant Brazil, one of the best in his field, see also the imprint.

In short, my aim was to bring joy and, above all, to inspire readers/listeners with this collection of songs to engage with the subject again or more. Eternity is eternal, but our time is too limited to miss out on good music – everyone determines what is good for themselves (except for right-wing bullshit, which doesn't deserve the term "music").
Keep on rockin'!

Appendix: Title – Artist

Appendix: Artist (without title)
(First name first, band/group names without "The")

Ferdinand Köther

The author

... was born in the founding year of the Federal Republic of Germany, experienced his "big bang" in 1962/63 with the first songs of the Beatles, and since then, music has never let go of him, accompanying him through an extremely eventful life.
He presents 100 of these lifelong companions here.

Rock 'n' Roll Never Dies!